Dee Brown

Hear That Lonesome Whistle Blow

Railroads in the West

Pan Books London and Sydney

First published in Great Britain 1977 by Chatto & Windus Ltd
This edition published 1979 by Pan Books Ltd,
Cavaye Place, London SW10 9PG
© Dee Brown 1977
ISBN 0 330 25656 4
Printed and bound in Great Britain by
Richard Clay (The Chaucer Press) Ltd, Bungay, Suffolk

We do not ride on the railroad; it rides upon us. Did you ever think what those sleepers are that underlie the railroad? Each one is a man, an Irishman, or a Yankee man. THOREAU

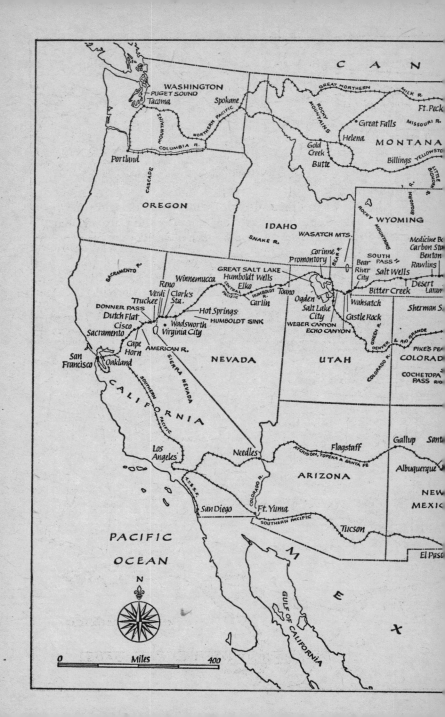

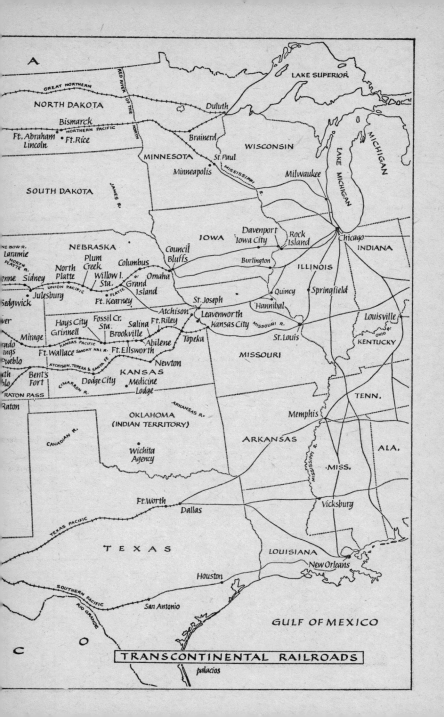

TRANSCONTINENTAL RAILROADS

palacios

Contents

ONE

The Iron Horse Comes to the Waters of the Mighty Mississippi

'Amid the acclamations of a multitude that no man could number, and the roar of artillery, making the very heavens tremble, punctual to the moment, the Iron Horse appeared in sight, rolling with a slow yet mighty motion to the depot. After him followed a train of six passenger cars crammed to the utmost with proud and joyful guests, with waving flags and handkerchiefs, and whose glad voices re-echoed back the roar of greeting with which they were received. Then came another locomotive and train of five passenger cars, equally crowded and decorated. This splendid pageant came to a stop in front of the depot, and the united cheers of the whole proclaimed to the world that the end was attained, and the Chicago & Rock Island Railway was opened through for travel and business.'

In 1854 many Americans were alive who had been born in the lifetime of George Washington, and celebrations of his birthday were still occasions of patriotic rejoicing and respect. That was why the builders of the first railroad from the East to reach the Mississippi River seized upon 22 February as the day to celebrate the 'nuptial feast of the great Atlantic Ocean to the mighty Father of Waters'. The track layers worked overtime to complete the final link, and the last rail was spiked to the ties only an hour before the Chicago & Rock Island's Locomotive No. 10, decorated with wreaths, garlands, and patriotic bunting, came whistling into view of the great river.

Rock Island, Illinois, was a town of between four and five thousand, a rival of Davenport across on the Iowa bank. The towns lived off steamboating, and numerous citizens of both communities hated railroads because of their threat to the thriving steamboat monopoly that dominated the Mississippi and its tributaries. It had been the same back in the East – rivermen, canalers, and wagoners all feared and hated the railroads that kept moving westward. And now at Rock Island the iron tracks had reached the river heart of the republic. The Iron Horse was the marvel of the age, a metal monster panting as though energized with the forces of life, exhaling steam and smoke, its centred oil headlight reminding some observers of the one-eyed cannibal giants of Homer – the Cyclops. To those more familiar with biblical references, the engine was Behemoth, its bones strong pieces of brass and bars of iron, and it could draw up the Mississippi into its mouth.

The presence of Locomotive No. 10 on the bank of the great river that day portended more than any man or woman there could have dreamed of. Its Cyclopean eye faced westward to the undulating land that flowed into a grassed horizon and curved over the limitless expanse of the Great Plains a thousand miles to a harsh upthrust of Shining Mountains, the Rockies, and then down to the Western Sea – that goal of European wanderers and seekers across North America for three centuries, the great ocean that Ferdinand Magellan named the Pacific.

Since the coming of the Europeans, the pioneers pushing always westward had been bound by waterways; the settlements they built were strung along the water routes like successive beads. Beyond the Mississippi, the Missouri River was the way West. Since Lewis and Clark, traders had marked overland trails to Santa Fe for trade with the Spaniards, to Oregon for furs, and to California for gold. Yet, compared to river commerce, the overland wagon caravans were insignificant. Away from the rivers few towns flourished. The American West was a vast and virginal land, awesome, beautiful, unbounded, and filled with immeasurable riches above and below the ground. Its ecosystem was a delicate balance of animals, grasses, shrubs, trees, and streams, with several dozen native civilizations – the American Indian tribes – blending into the whole. Even as late as the middle of the nineteenth century, the white invaders had brought no more change to the Western land than might have been accomplished by a handful of ants. Their puny wagon trains and their steamboats struggling against the Missouri currents left but slight traces of their passage. Even in the California goldfields, the seekers of wealth were as pygmies in a giant's land, building and abandoning camps in their restless searches, the wounded earth healing itself behind them.

Only the demonic power of the Iron Horse and its bands of iron track could conquer the West, and on this cold sunlit February day in 1854, Locomotive No. 10 stood on the edge of the frontier, softly breathing smoke and steam while its load of rejoicing passengers detrained to celebrate. An awaiting group of musicians struck up 'Hail, Columbia', and the local dignitaries and those who had come from the East pushed into the spacious new depot where banquet tables awaited them.

The speakers that day were well aware that the occasion they celebrated was epochal. The human race had moved itself another notch forward in its long quest for the Western Sea. 'If the roar of artillery and the scream of the Iron Horse which are now awakening the echoes of the Mississippi Valley,' said one, 'could alone awaken the spirits of departed pioneers, what would they now behold! In the place of the immigrant wagon, conveying his single family, he would witness a vehicle conveying a family of cities, and drawn by an agent more powerful than Behemoth himself. He would be told that where he took months to perform his journey it was now done in a less number of days.' Numerous references were made to the 'iron steed' following the Star of Empire, to bands of iron binding ocean to river, and to the marking of an era in the history of the world's progress. One speaker compared the event to Venice's annual espousal with the Adriatic in celebration of that city's commercial prosperity.

As was the custom of the times, toasts were offered to everybody from George Washington down to the lowliest local politician. They toasted 'the Press, the Telegraph and the Steam Engine, the three levers which move the world of modern civilization'. The governor of Illinois toasted his state and eulogized the West, predicting that 'the child is now living who will see this continent inhabited by four hundred millions of people, three hundred millions of which will be found in the Mississippi Valley.' Fortunately, the governor was wrong; otherwise, his descendants in the late twentieth century would be living under population conditions similar to those of Asia. For years, however, the opening of new railroads would inspire politicians to orate upon the glories of unlimited growth.

After each toast, a man stationed near the depot entrance would signal the engineer on the Iron Horse outside to applaud with an ear-splitting blast from the whistle. And then the lively brass band would follow with a few bars from its favourite new march tune, 'The Railroad Quickstep'.

Excepting the long-winded and now long-forgotten politicians, the hero of the day was Henry Farnam, a forty-nine-year-old Easterner who had brought the first railroad into Chicago two years earlier and who was largely responsible for the building of the Chicago & Rock Island. A descendant of New England pioneers, Farnam was an earnest, strong-jawed, clear-eyed man who believed in honesty and hard work. Like the youthful Abraham Lincoln, he had read and studied by the dancing light of an open fireplace. After teaching himself mathematics he became a surveyor, got into canal building, and then foresaw the future and switched to railroads.

In the Rock Island depot that evening when Farnam was called upon to speak, he responded briefly, giving his associates most of the credit for completion of the railroad and expressing mild amazement over the rapidity with which the Iron Horse had crossed half the continent. Among his associates were four men whose names would become well known to most Americans during the next decade, when the building of the first transcontinental railroad attracted national attention. They were Thomas Clark Durant, skilful promoter of stocks and bonds; Peter Anthony Dey, surveyor and locating engineer; Grenville Mellen Dodge, who was Dey's assistant; and Samuel Benedict Reed, construction engineer. They all were vigorous young men, their ages ranging from the early twenties to middle thirties, and like Farnam they were Easterners from New England and New York State. Together they possessed a store of hard experience at canal and railroad building and financing. Dey and Dodge were already in Iowa, surveying a line westward, and Durant was negotiating for stock sales and land grants to construct a railroad from Davenport on the Mississippi to Council Bluffs on the Missouri. Soon they would change the name of the Chicago & Rock Island to the Chicago, Rock Island & *Pacific* Railroad. The CRI & P would never reach that Western Sea on its own tracks, but many of the men who built the Rock Island would be in the forefront of the great transcontinental railroad race.

After the banquet was ended that evening, Henry Farnam and his friends walked along the streets of Rock Island town. The dwellings and public houses were brilliantly illuminated to honour the great occasion, and across the dark river the lights of Davenport were equally bright. It was towards the West that the railroad builders' thoughts were inclined to run. None of them realized that they had fixed the destiny of Chicago as the railroad centre of the continent and had guaranteed that the port city of New York would now become the commercial centre of the young republic. The citizens of New Orleans had yearned for that power, built upon water traffic, and St Louisans had dreamed of creating a Queen City of rivers and railroads extending to lakes and oceans and gulf. But in Council Bluffs, the friends and associates of the firm of Farnam & Durant were already arranging for establishment of an incorporated town directly across the Missouri River in Nebraska Territory. Out of a rude collection of ramshackle dwellings, livery stables, fur-trading posts, and grog shops, they created a town to ensure that the railroad from the East would be logically impelled to cross the Missouri at that point and continue towards the Western Sea. On land taken from the ten clans of the Omaha nation of Indians, the new town was named for that dispossessed tribe, a precedent in railroad building that would continue across the West for another generation. Farnam and Durant were now ready to extend their railroad across Iowa. At the same time, they had to construct a connecting bridge, the first such structure to span the broad Mississippi.

It was mainly because of the island – Rock Island – in the middle of the river that Farnam and his locating engineers had chosen the town of that name to be the river terminus of their railroad. A bridge there, they reasoned, would be easier and less costly to construct and should offer a minimum hazard to steamboat navigation. Yet, before construction could begin, loud outcries arose from steamboat owners in St Louis who saw the railroad as a threat to their booming freight monopoly. They charged that the bridge was 'unconstitutional, an obstruction to navigation, dangerous, and it was the duty of every western state, river city, and town to take immediate action to prevent the erection of such a structure'. As soon as Farnam's Railroad Bridge Company began construction of piers and the first superstructure, a stronger opposition came from Southern sectionalists, who for a decade had been fighting to ensure that the first transcontinental railroad would originate in the slave-holding South and cross the southern half of the country. Leader of this opposition was none other than Jefferson Davis, who seven years later, at the beginning of the Civil War, would become President of the seceding Confederate States of America. In 1854, Davis was in a strategic position to block the bridge; he was Secretary of War, and because the island in the Mississippi had once been used as a military reservation he informed Farnam's railroad company that Rock Island could not be used in construction of a river bridge.

Encouraged by this official contravention, the steamboat interests late in 1854 secured a federal injunction that charged the bridge builders with illegal trespassing, destruction of government property, and obstruction of steamboat navigation. When the case was brought to court in July 1855, however, the judge ruled for the Railroad Bridge Company, declaring that the bridge was not an obstruction to navigation and that 'railroads had become highways in something the same sense as rivers; neither could be suffered to become a permanent obstruction to the other, but each must yield something to the other according to the demands of the public convenience and necessities of commerce'.

Nine months later, Farnam's 1,535-foot-long bridge was completed, and on 22 April 1856, he was one of the passengers on the first train approaching it from the East. A newspaper correspondent described the crossing:

Swiftly we sped along the iron track – Rock Island appeared in sight – the whistle sounded and the conductor cried out: *'Passengers for Iowa keep their seats.'* There was a pause – a hush, as it were, preparatory to the fierceness of a tornado. The cars moved on – the bridge was reached – 'We're on the bridge – see the mighty Mississippi rolling on beneath'

– and all eyes were fastened on the mighty parapets of the magnificent bridge, over which we glided in solemn silence. A few minutes and the suspended breath was let loose. 'We're over,' was the cry. 'We have cross the Mississippi in a railroad car.' 'This is glory enough for one day,' said a passenger, as he hustled his carpet bag and himself out of the car. We followed, to view the mighty structure.

In Davenport and Rock Island, church bells began ringing and crowds that had gathered along both banks of the river broke into enthusiastic cheers. Telegraphers flashed the news back to cities in the East, where it created much excitement. 'Civilization took a railroad trip across the Mississippi,' declared the *Philadelphia Bulletin*. 'The great bridge over the great river ... was completed and a train of cars passed over it, carrying a load of passengers – commonplace passengers enough, perhaps, but passengers who will always look back exultingly and toast to their children and grandchildren that they were in the first train of cars that ever crossed the Mississippi.' Like most Americans, the Philadelphia editor had his eye on the Western Sea: 'Now that civilization has got safely over the Mississippi by steam, we see no reason why we may not live to see her take a first class ticket in a lightning train for the shores of the Pacific.' He ended by predicting that 'twenty years hence' railroad men would be tunnelling the Rocky Mountains. His estimate was conservative; in less than ten years track crews would be blasting tunnels through the Rockies.

If Farnam and Durant believed their troubles with the Mississippi rivermen were behind them, they must have suffered a sharp jolt a few days later. Early on the morning of 6 May, a persistent blowing of steamboat whistles and ringing of alarm bells brought the townspeople of Rock Island and Davenport out of their houses. Black smoke was boiling skyward from the new bridge. Just after dawn, the packet boat *Effie Afton*, out of New Orleans, had collided broadside against the bridge, the crash knocking down her chimneys and overturning her stoves, which set the vessel afire. Within minutes the blaze spread to a wooden section of the bridge, and while crowds watched from the bridge ends, one flaming span fell into the river. Both boat and bridge span went floating away with the current.

Up and down the Mississippi that morning, steamboat captains blew triumphant blasts on their whistles, arousing railroad partisans' suspicions that the collision had been intentional, that the *Effie Afton* had been sacrificed for the purpose of destroying the bridge. And they must have been convinced of a plot by the rivermen when the steamboat *Hamburg* raised a large banner that read: MISSISSIPPI BRIDGE DESTROYED. LET ALL REJOICE.

Believing that they now had the railroad company on the run, the steamboat interests opened a barrage of public attacks upon Farnam's Railroad Bridge Company. In St Louis, rivermen and businessmen passed a joint resolution to take all necessary legal steps to have the bridge removed. A committee of steamboat pilots and captains inspected the bridge and solemnly reported that the structure was 'a great and serious obstacle to navigation'. And then the owner of the *Effie Afton* brought a heavy damage suit against the bridge company, charging that, among other things, the presence of the piers created a swift river current that had swept the packet boat out of control.

Farnam and his associates immediately sought out a first-rate lawyer, one who had a reputation for winning most of his cases. They found him in Springfield, Illinois, and his name was Abraham Lincoln.

Meanwhile, the railroad owners ignored the attacks upon their bridge and began rebuilding the burned section, putting it back into service in September. They also investigated the reasons for the *Effie Afton*'s presence at Rock Island; the boat's usual run was between New Orleans and Louisville and there was no explanation for her being in the upper Mississippi. Had the packet boat been rerouted purposely to destroy the bridge? Was the vessel loaded with inflammable materials? Nothing could be proved.

The case was long delayed in coming to court. On 1 September 1857, Abraham Lincoln visited Rock Island and made a personal inspection of the scene of the collision. He questioned the bridge master and several steamboat pilots and river engineers, and then after gathering all the information he could in this way, he walked out onto the bridge and sat on one of its stringers for an hour or so, studying the currents. With the assistance of a teen-aged boy named Ben Brayton, he determined the speed and direction of the currents by timing with his silver watch the movement of logs and brush that young Brayton dropped into the stream.

A week later, what was to become known as the landmark Rock Island Bridge Case opened sessions in the Saloon Building at Clark and Lake streets in Chicago. It soon became evident to spectators that what they were watching was a struggle between the economic forces of the North and those of the South. A victory for the steamboat interests would mean that the corn and wheat, the pork and timber – all the abundance of the burgeoning Midwest – would continue to move southward along the rivers. St Louis, Memphis, and New Orleans would become the national centres of trade. On the other hand, a victory for the railroads would mean that commerce could move east and west in a steadily growing volume and thereby assure the destinies of Chicago and New York.

As the trial proceeded, a parade of boat owners, pilots, engineers, and bridge builders passed through the courtroom to be questioned and cross-questioned. During the first days, Lincoln spent much of his time sitting on a bench whittling, but when he did rise to challenge a witness he displayed an enormous fund of information about the measurements of the bridge, the exact lengths of spans, the water's depth, and the dimensions of the *Effie Afton*. At that time he was in his early forties; he wore a dark bush of hair and was clean-shaven. His control of the defence, 'his clear statements and choice logic', and his frontier humour, which seemed so incongruous with his solemn and preoccupied appearance, won him a considerable amount of attention in the Chicago press and among men of power who two years later would push him into the race for President of the United States.

In his closing argument to the jury, Lincoln's knowledge of the river currents – gained with the help of young Ben Brayton – enabled him to demolish one of the principal points of the plaintiffs. Using models of the *Effie Afton* and the bridge, he demonstrated that the starboard wheel of the steamboat could not have been operating at the time of the accident. 'The fact is undisputed that she did not move one inch ahead while she was moving thirty-one feet sideways. There is evidence proving that the current there is *only five miles an hour*, and the only explanation is that her power was not all used – that only one wheel was working.'

The theme that Lincoln emphasized repeatedly in his argument was that railroads had as much right to cross rivers as steamboats had to travel up and down them, and that travel between the East and the West was as important as between the North and the South. 'Mr Lincoln in addressing the court,' said one observer, 'claimed that rivers were to be crossed and that it was the manifest destiny of the people to move westward and surround themselves with everything connected with modern civilization.'

Although the jurors failed to reach a decision and were dismissed, the railway people knew they had won a great victory. Steamboat supporters who had travelled from St Louis, New Orleans, and other river cities went home disappointed and embittered, but were determined to continue their fight against the Rock Island bridge and any like it. In 1858 they tried – and failed – to secure congressional passage of a law forbidding bridges over navigable rivers. Later in that same year they finally won a battle in an Iowa court, the judge declaring the Rock Island bridge 'a common and public nuisance' and ordering removal of 'the three piers and their superstructure which lie within the State of Iowa'.

The Chicago & Rock Island appealed to the Supreme Court, where at last the right of railroads to bridge rivers was settled legally forever. For some years afterwards, however, whenever a new railroad bridge was built across a navigable river, mysterious accidents often occurred. And at least one more attempt was made to destroy the Rock Island bridge. On the night of 5 June 1859, a watchman making his rounds of inspection found in the middle of the bridge a collection of gunpowder, tar, oakum, and brimstone, heaped up and ready to be set on fire.

In the meantime, out upon the rolling plains of Iowa, Peter Dey and his young assistant, Grenville Dodge, had been making preliminary surveys for a railroad to run between Davenport on the Mississippi and Council Bluffs on the Missouri. Although this railroad across Iowa was to be built, owned, and operated by the same men who controlled the Chicago & Rock Island, they established the new company as a separate organization and named it the Mississippi & Missouri Railroad.

This was done mainly for financial reasons, and in the mind of Thomas Durant the making of money was the only reason why a man should spend his time and energies at railroad building. Pride of accomplishment, the excitement of opening new frontiers, and fulfilling society's need for transportation meant nothing to him. A photograph taken of Durant at about this time shows him seated at a table, happily totalling up figures on a long scroll of paper. Although he had graduated with honours from a medical college, he had become bored with medicine and had turned to making fortunes by speculating in grain futures and railroad stocks. Yet he still liked to be called 'Doctor' Durant.

None of the officers of the M & M was more pleased than Durant that General John Adams Dix had agreed to serve as president of the company. Dix had been a US senator, knew his way around the founts of political power in the East, and had managed to establish an image as an honest politician, which was as much of a rarity then as now. Dix's main function was to help the company in its efforts to secure federal land grants, and he was therefore only a nominal president. Henry Farnam, under the title of 'chief engineer', performed most of the presidential duties in Iowa while Dix lobbied in Washington. As for Durant, his self-chosen task was to negotiate securities in New York and to direct field agents in efforts to persuade Iowa counties and towns to issue bonds and subscribe to stock.

To start the roadbed grading, Farnam assembled at Davenport six hundred labourers – mostly Irish immigrants – and in June 1855 they began laying tracks. 'British iron', Farnam called these first rails, which had been shipped all the way from iron foundries in Great Britain. A month later, the M & M's first locomotive arrived. As the Rock Island bridge was not then completed, the Iron Horse had to be floated over on a flatboat ingeniously rigged with a temporary track from which the locomotive could be rolled onto a spur line and then up to the Davenport station.

The first locomotive was named 'Antoine Le Claire' in honour of the son of a French fur trader and a Potawatomi princess. Le

Claire was one of the founders of Davenport – a booster for the railroad – and had donated his townhouse for conversion into a luxurious railroad station. In the 1850s, new locomotives were as gaily painted and decorated as new stagecoaches, and the resplendent 'Antoine Le Claire' also bore upon its side panels two bronze bas-relief statues of the man for whom it was named.

While a large crowd was gathering to admire the new locomotive, the engineer and fireman filled its boiler with water and its firebox with scrap lumber from a nearby saw-mill. When the monster came to steaming life, the engineer invited spectators to climb aboard for the trial run. Among those who responded with delight was a group of Antoine Le Claire's Indian relatives and friends whose blankets were as brilliantly coloured as the Iron Horse that had intruded upon their lost land. 'They swarmed upon and over her, a score of them,' reported an observer, 'and so, with all the passengers, red and white, that could be stuck on the tender and the cab, the first run in this section of the United States was made.'

Iowans now bestowed upon Henry Farnam the title of 'Farnam the Railroad King'. Almost every day he was out with his workmen, driving them until they completed at least half a mile of track each day. At the same time, his partner Durant was busily converting the local excitement into money. As the rails moved westward, a surefire moneymaking device was to lay out town lots adjacent to the approaching railroad line and then auction them off to settlers pouring into the empty land. (Half a million people followed the railroads into Iowa during the 1850s.)

Land only a few miles distant from the line survey was so much cheaper than land adjoining it that the sly moneymaker, Dr Durant, bought up sections of distant acreage and then persuaded Farnam to abandon the original survey and shift the railroad northward so as to strike holdings. He named a town site after himself, and funnelled the lucrative receipts from lot sales back to his accounts in New York. It was a typical Durant manoeuvre; he had no further interest in the town, which 120 years later had attracted less than fifteen hundred inhabitants.

Meanwhile, thirty miles to the west, the citizens of Iowa City, apparently fearful that the M & M might veer off in some other direction, hurriedly raised fifty thousand dollars which they promised the railroad as a prize if it could bring an Iron Horse into their town before 1 January 1856. In 1855, fifty thousand dollars was a fortune, and Farnam accepted the challenge. Although rain and cold weather slowed his track layers, he was within three miles of Iowa City on Christmas Day. Temperatures of zero and below, however, threatened to defeat him. Ice formed in locomotive boilers, and the workmen complained of frostbite.

On New Year's Eve, with the deadline only a few hours away, the end of the track was still several hundred feet from the Iowa City depot. Farnam ordered huge bonfires built along the right-of-way to furnish warmth and light, and he employed every man in Iowa City who was willing to work. The locomotive crawled to within two hundred feet of the station and then its boiler froze. Farnam set his trainmen to using pinch bars, and inch by inch they propelled the Iron Horse forward until it stood at track's end beside the station platform. A few minutes afterwards, church bells began ringing to signal the new year of 1856. Three days later, with the temperature still well below zero, the first regularly scheduled passenger train rolled in from Davenport. Aboard was a huge shipment of fresh oysters, the first ever to arrive in the heart of Iowa. That evening Henry Farnam spent a considerable part of his fifty-thousand-dollar prize on a feast for all the people of Iowa City, serving them hot coffee, cake, and oysters 'till broad daylight in the morning'.

During the following year, Dr Durant increased his efforts to persuade the villages and counties between Iowa City and the Missouri River to pledge more railroad bonds. He was aided in this campaign by Northern antislavery forces who were aroused over passage of the Kansas-Nebraska Act. This law, which created the new territories of Kansas and Nebraska, included a provision for settlers of the territories to decide for themselves whether they would allow slavery within their borders. A fierce immigration race had already begun between pro-slavery settlers from the South and anti-slavery settlers from the North, thus putting in motion a series of events that would soon lead to the first violent clashes of the oncoming Civil War.

'We advocate the building of this railroad earnestly as a peace measure,' argued a Chicago newspaper editor. 'The very announcement that the stock was subscribed and that the road was to be finished by the 4th of July, 1858, would at once settle this question.' He predicted that anti-slavery immigrants would pour into the territories on the new railroad and the freedom of Kansas and Nebraska would be assured. Moreover, the railroad's stock was an excellent investment, paying perhaps twelve per cent dividends.

None of this sectional rivalry was lost upon the railroad operators. After the Rock Island bridge was completed, they began advertising their two routes as 'the great national road to Kansas and Nebraska'. In that same year, the lobbying efforts of General John Dix in Washington paid off when Congress voted an Iowa land-grant act that guaranteed thousands of acres to the railroad builders. This was what Durant had hungered for, and as soon as the M & M had 400,000 acres of rich Iowa soil in its grab bag, he deliberately schemed to slow the building of the road. The land-grant act generously allowed ten years for the road's completion, and there were special taxation privileges. The longer the road was delayed, the more valuable the land grants would become, and the more eager the settlers to the West would be to increase the size of their stock and bond commitments in hopes of bringing the Iron Horse to their towns.

Although he did not fully understand what his partner was doing, honest Henry Farnam began to distrust Durant's policies and manipulations. 'Durant,' he said afterwards, 'unfortunately yielded to the general spirit of speculation which had taken possession of so many railroad men of that time.' Farnam believed it was his duty to build the railroad as quickly and efficiently as possible. When Durant squeezed down on funds for road construction, Farnam recklessly spent some of his own money to buy materials and meet payrolls. In August 1857, a financial crisis in the East gave Durant and his New York associates an opportunity to order Farnam to cease all work on the M & M. By this time, Farnam's distaste for Durant's business ethics reached the point where he could no longer continue in partnership with him. The firm of Farnam & Durant was dissolved, Farnam retaining his post as president of the Rock Island

Railroad until Durant's power reached the point where he could force him out of that office and replace him with his brother, Charles Durant.

Thomas Durant scorned men who built railroads for the joy of building and whose moral principles got in the way of their profits. After he was rid of Henry Farnam, Durant enjoyed himself manipulating the farmers and villagers of Iowa, threatening to bypass towns or counties that did not buy more bonds, generating rumours that he would run his railroad north of Council Bluffs, bridge the Missouri at another location, and create a rival city to Omaha. As a result, many towns and counties voted bonds out of all proportion to their ability to pay, saddling their people with heavy debts for years into the future. For this, Durant offered no guarantees, and was not even liable for defaults if he failed to build tracks along original surveys.

When another railroad, the Chicago & Northwestern, began crossing Iowa through a tier of countries north of the M & M, Durant did not respond with a track-laying race. The C & N reached Council Bluffs two years before the plodding M & M (which by then had been combined into the Chicago, Rock Island & Pacific Railroad), and one of Durant's employees, surveyor Grenville Dodge, was the principal speaker at the banquet arranged to welcome the builders of the supposed 'rival' railroad. Few people knew, or cared, that the president of the Chicago & Northwestern was also vice-president of the Mississippi & Missouri, or that Dr Durant had exploited the latter road almost into bankruptcy, sold his stock at a profit, and reinvested in the C & N.

The whole affair, of course, was but a rehearsal for that 'Grandest Enterprise Under God', the building of the first transcontinental railroad, the route to the Indies by way of the Western Sea.

TWO

'With the Wings of the Wind'

'Less than a quarter of a century ago,' said Henry Farnam, 'the first locomotive was introduced into the United States. Now, more than fourteen thousand miles of iron rails are traversed by the Iron Horse with almost lightning speed.' Farnam was responding to a toast given at the celebration that united the Atlantic with the Mississippi at Rock Island, Illinois, on Washington's birthday, 1854. The first Iron Horse had arrived in America almost exactly a quarter of a century earlier, in May 1829. In August of the same year it was given a trial run on a track near Honesdale, Pennsylvania. During that brief span of years (1829–54) the development of locomotives and the building of tracks for them to run upon had been amazingly swift, even more so than was to be the development of automobiles and paved highways in the twentieth century.

In the first years of the nineteenth century, many Americans were keenly interested in reports from England that told of astounding progress in the use of steam-propelled engines. These were used mainly to replace horses, which for years had been drawing wagons loaded with coal over railways that ran from colliery pit-heads to shipping ports. In 1813, Americans heard about William Hedley's 'Puffing Billy', which could haul ten coal wagons at five miles per hour. In 1825, they marvelled over George Stephenson's 'Locomotion', which reached a speed of sixteen miles per hour on the new Stockton and Darlington railway. Four years later, Stephenson and his son perfected the 'Rocket', with its multi-tube boiler and improved system of exhausting steam, which created a strong draught in the firebox. The 'Rocket' was the first true, breathing, pure-bred Iron Horse, and could travel twenty-nine miles in one hour.

During this same period in America a number of imaginative people were planning railways – from New York to Philadelphia, from Baltimore to the West, from Albany to Lake Erie, from Charleston, South Carolina, to the West. In most cases, the planning did not include the use of steam power; the cars would be pulled by horses, as was done on the short lines that ran from coal mines to canals or rivers. In 1825, Colonel John Stevens demonstrated a one-cylinder steam-powered locomotive on a circular track on the grounds of his estate in Hoboken, New Jersey, but the public viewed it as an amusing toy. Not until 1828 did a trained engineer travel to England to examine the marvellous Iron Horse at work.

Horatio Allen was his name, and he was sent on his mission by John B. Jervis of the Delaware & Hudson Canal Company. (Less than a quarter of a century later, Jervis was serving as the first president of his friend Henry Farnam's Chicago & Rock Island Railroad.) Jervis authorized the twenty-five-year-old Allen to buy iron to replace wooden rails on the canal's horse-powered railways. In addition to the rails, if Allen discovered that the much-publicized English locomotives were as practical as they were said to be, he was to buy four of them.

Much impressed by what he saw, young Allen placed orders for four Iron Horses, and on 13 May 1829, the first English locomotive arrived in New York City. According to one observer, it resembled a mammoth grasshopper. 'Its driving wheels were of oak-wood, banded with a heavy wrought-iron tire, and the front was ornamented with a large, fierce-looking face of a lion, in bold relief, and it bore the name of "Stourbridge Lion".' It was a four-wheeled engine with a cylindrical boiler, and had been built by Foster, Rastrick & Company at Stourbridge, England. Allen arranged to have the 'Lion' blocked up in a New York foundry yard and there he brought it to life with steam, and 'it became the object of curiosity to thousands who visited the works from day to day, to see the curious "critter" go through the motions only, as there was no road for it about the premises.'

In July, Allen shipped the locomotive by river and canal to Honesdale, Pennsylvania, and there on 8 August a fire was kindled under the boiler, and the 'Stourbridge Lion' was readied for its first test. The railway that ran to the coal mines at Carbondale was made of hemlock timber that had cracked and warped from exposure, and after a straight section of five hundred feet it crossed Lackawaxen Creek on a curved trestlework about thirty feet high.

'The impression was very general,' Horatio Allen recalled afterwards, 'that the iron monster would either break down the road or that it would leave the track at the curve and plunge into the creek. My reply to such apprehension was, that it was too late to consider the probability of such occurrences; that there was no other course but to have the trial made of the strange animal which had been brought here at such great expense, but that it was not necessary that more than one should be involved in its fate; that I would take the first ride alone, and that the time would come when I should look back to this incident with great interest. As I placed my hand on the throttle-valve handle I was undecided whether I would move slowly or with a fair degree of speed; but believing that the road would prove safe, and preferring, if we did go down, to go down handsomely and without any evidence of timidity, I started with considerable velocity, passed the curve over the creek safely, and was soon out of hearing of the cheers of the large assemblage present. At the end of two or three miles, I reversed the valves and returned without accident to the place of starting, having thus made the first railroad trip by locomotive on the Western Hemisphere.'

Only a year later, Peter Cooper took the first locomotive built in America out for a trial run on the Baltimore & Ohio's recently completed thirteen miles of track between Baltimore and Ellicott's Mills in Maryland. Appropriately named 'Tom Thumb', the locomotive was built by Cooper as a working model meant to convert the railroad's directors from their hidebound preference for horse-power over steam-power. On 28 August 1830, Cooper attached 'Tom Thumb' to a car that resembled an open boat. It was crowded with beaver-hatted directors and their friends. Thus began the first journey by steam in America aboard an American-built locomotive. On the run to Ellicott's Mills, Cooper's passengers were delighted when he easily maintained speeds of fifteen to eighteen miles per hour, but on the return trip a horse-drawn car was waiting to challenge him at Relay House, from which point parallel tracks ran to Baltimore. Stockton & Stokes, stagecoach operators and advocates of horse-drawn rail cars, insisted that 'Tom Thumb' engage in a race, and Cooper accepted. The horse leaped away into the lead, but 'Tom Thumb' quickly overtook the animal and passed it with a burst of speed. A few minutes later, just as the driver of the horse was about to abandon the contest, the blower belt slipped from 'Tom Thumb's' drum.

'The safety-valve ceased to scream,' reported one of the passengers, 'and the engine for want of breath began to wheeze and pant. In vain Mr Cooper, who was his own engineer and fireman, lacerated his hand in attempting to replace the band upon the wheel; in vain he tried to urge the fire with light wood. The horse gained on the machine and passed it, and, although the band was presently replaced, and steam again did its best, the horse was too far ahead to be overtaken, and came in the winner of the race.' Although Peter Cooper lost the race, he won his battle for steam-power. 'Tom Thumb's' performance convinced the directors of the Baltimore & Ohio that they should bet their money on the Iron Horse. They announced a contest for a locomotive especially designed for their steeply graded and sharply curved railroad that was to be built through the Allegheny Mountains.

In the meantime, Horatio Allen – that dauntless driver of the 'Stourbridge Lion' – had transferred his engineering skills to a new railroad that was being built westward from Charleston, South Carolina. Collaborating with one of the road's directors, he helped design a new locomotive, which was named 'Best Friend of Charleston'. The leading citizens of Charleston were determined that their city should become America's greatest seaport, and to achieve this aim they envisioned a railroad with many branches bringing into their harbour the rich produce of the South and the West. 'Best Friend of Charleston', which had a vertical boiler shaped like a wine bottle, was America's first regularly scheduled passenger-train locomotive and it operated over what was then the longest railroad in the world. Unfortunately, on 17 June 1831, the 'Best Friend's' fireman – who evidently underestimated the power of steam – became annoyed by the hissing of the safety valve and tied down the lever. The result was another 'first' for 'Best Friend'. It was the first locomotive to explode, an accident that killed the fireman and badly scalded the engineer. Horatio Allen's mechanics managed to rebuild what was left of the locomotive, and it was appropriately rechristened 'Phoenix'. To restore the confidence of passengers on the Charleston & Hamburg Railroad, a flatcar heaped high with protective cotton bales was thereafter placed between the locomotive and its passenger cars – a practice that was continued for many years.

In the 1830s it seemed that every blacksmith, tinker, and ironworker, every wagonwright, carriagesmith, and boilermaker – all the craftsmen of America – wanted to build a better locomotive. Among those drawn to the romance of the Iron Horse was a Philadelphia jeweller and bookbinder, Matthias William Baldwin. In 1831 he built a miniature steam locomotive for the Philadelphia Museum, and its efficiency so impressed the owners of the newly founded Philadelphia, Germantown & Norristown Railroad that they commissioned him to build a full-sized Iron Horse for a promised payment of four thousand dollars.

Before beginning work, Baldwin visited Colonel John Stevens's Camden & Amboy Railroad and made a thorough examination of the 'John Bull', a recent import from the famed Stephensons' works in Newcastle, England. On 23 November 1832, Baldwin's 'Old Ironsides' was ready for a test run. After correcting some imperfections, Baldwin turned the locomotive over to the railroad, expecting to receive the four thousand dollars. The company, however, complained that 'Old Ironsides' did not meet their expectations. It could be used when the weather was fair, they said, but horses had to be substituted when the weather was poor. They finally settled for thirty-five hundred dollars; and the disgusted Matthias Baldwin told his mechanics: 'That is our last locomotive.'

The lure of the Iron Horse was too great, however, and Baldwin was soon at work on the 'E. L. Miller' for the Charleston & Hamburg Railroad. Before he died in 1866 he personally supervised the building of fifteen hundred locomotives, and the company that bore his name built fifty-nine thousand Iron Horses before it was absorbed into a corporate conglomerate of the twentieth century.

By the 1840s, Baldwin and other locomotive builders of America and Britain had transformed the original crude machine into the powerful Behemoth that would change the face of the earth. The vertical wine-bottle boiler became horizontal; flanges were placed on the wheels instead of on the tracks; flexible beam trucks were designed to prevent binding or derailment when the engine rounded curves; a pilot or cowcatcher was placed on the prow; a weatherproof cab sheltered the engineer and fireman from the elements; flared spark-arresting smokestacks shaped like balloons, sunflowers, and cabbage heads replaced the straight stacks; boxed oil headlamps embellished with elaborate designs made night travel possible; brass-capped domes filled with sand to give traction to spinning wheels appeared behind the smokestacks; mellow-toned bells and melodious whistles added both safety and charm.

It was no wonder that when Americans were swept up in their national drive towards the Western Sea – their mania for Manifest Destiny – they looked upon the Iron Horse as 'the wings of the wind', which would take them where they desired to go. In 1846, that Year of Decision when Americans moved to seize California, Oregon Territory, and much of the Southwest, locomotives and the recently invented telegraph figured largely in much of the bombastic oratory. For example, Congressman Charles W. Cathcart of Indiana, speaking on the floor of the House of Representatives, 6 February 1846: 'The Iron Horse [the steamcar] with the wings of the wind, his nostrils distended with flame, salamander-like vomiting fire and smoke, trembling with power, but submissive to the steel curb imposed upon him by the hand of man, flies from one end of the continent to the other in less time than our ancestry required to visit a neighbouring city; while by the magnetic telegraph the lightning of heaven is made subservient to the will of man in annihilating space. In storm and darkness, in the heat of a torrid sun or the chilling blasts of a Siberian winter, this mystical symbol of man's intelligence speeds its onward way. Truly it may be said, that with the social influence of these two great inventions, all the people of this continent may be moulded to one mind.'

There were exceptions to this view, of course. Another orator predicted that railroads would 'leave the land despoiled, ruined, a desert where only sable buzzards shall wing their loathsome way to feed upon the carrion accomplished by the iron monster of the locomotive engine.' Few Americans, however, were exempt from the enchantment with the Iron Horse, not even Henry David Thoreau, the philosophic naturalist and recluse of Walden Pond, who abhorred expansionism and the war with Mexico, but who could say of the locomotives that passed on the Fitchburg Railroad: 'When I hear the Iron Horse make the hills echo with his snort like thunder, shaking the earth with his feet, and breathing fire and smoke from his nostrils (what kind of winged horse or fiery dragon they will put into the new mythology I don't know) it seems as if the earth had sent a race now worthy to inhabit it.' And Joaquin Miller, that wild and shaggy singer of the West, declared that there was more poetry in the rushing monster 'than in all the gory story of burning Troy'.

In the 1840s the locomotive reached its natural form, a configuration that would be refined through technology and expanded in size, yet was virtually the same machine that would dominate the rails for the next century. In that decade it seemed that every merchant, manufacturer, and visionary, every peddler, pitchman, and politician was planning or dreaming of a rail route to the Western Sea.

Typical of the visionaries was John Plumbe, a Welshman who came to the United States in 1821 at the age of twelve and a few years later was working as a railroad surveyor in Pennsylvania. Always restless and ambitious, Plumbe moved on west to Iowa Territory, read law, and became a prosecuting attorney in the frontier county of Dubuque. There he spent much of his time organizing public meetings and corresponding with congressmen in a campaign to build a railroad to the Western Sea. He may have been the first advocate of record for a transcontinental railroad, when in 1838 he sent a petition to Washington that brought ridicule from congressmen who said his proposal was as silly as asking the government 'to build a railroad to the moon'.

By the early 1840s, Plumbe was back in the East, where he somehow learned the new art of daguerreotypy. Four years before the great Mathew Brady entered the business, he opened a chain of studios from Boston to Washington. In Washington, Plumbe made the first photographs of the Capitol, the White House, and other buildings, and probably the first portraits of such famous Americans as Sam Houston, Henry Clay, John C. Calhoun, James K. Polk, and John Quincy Adams. Because only one copy could be made of a daguerreotype, he developed a method for reproducing lithographic copies on paper, a process that he called Plumbeotypy, but he never bothered to obtain a patent.

It was while he was in Washington that Plumbe became caught up in the transcontinental-railroad fever of the 1840s, and began travelling about the country trying to bring his dream to fruition. Because of his neglect, his daguerreotype studios went bankrupt, and he joined the California gold rush to recoup his fortune. John Plumbe found no gold; in fact, he spent most of his time in California trying to persuade the swarms of new residents there to join him in formulating plans for a railroad to link them with the Eastern states. By this time, the dream of the railroad had become an obsession he could not escape. In these later years of his life, Plumbe bore a curious resemblance to his contemporary Edgar Allan Poe – high forehead, down-curving moustache, brooding eyes. When he returned to Iowa in 1857 a defeated man, and found that others had stolen his dream and were bringing it to reality, he became so despondent that he committed suicide at the age of forty-six.

More practical than John Plumbe was Asa Whitney, a New England merchant whose resemblance to Napoleon Bonaparte was so marked that strangers often stared at him in amazement. Whitney conceived his plan for a transcontinental railroad while returning from a voyage to China in 1844. Five Chinese ports had recently (1843) been opened to trade, but Whitney was discouraged by the interminable sea distance from Boston or New York. A railroad across the North American continent seemed the best solution, and although rails had not then reached Chicago, Whitney began investigating possible routes from Lake Michigan to the Pacific Coast.

In 1845 Whitney addressed a memorial to Congress, recommending that a survey for a transcontinental railroad between the 42nd and 45th parallels be authorized as soon as possible. He then went on a tour of the country, making speeches, visiting community leaders, and writing letters to newspapers in efforts to drum up support for the railroad. In the summer of that year he organized an expedition at his own expense to explore a rail route towards the Western Sea. Starting at Milwaukee, he and his party of young adventurers crossed the prairies to the Great Bend of the Missouri. At every opportunity Whitney sent back lengthy reports to newspapers, extolling the richness of the country through which his railroad would pass and urging the government to complete his survey from the Missouri to the Pacific Coast. After returning to the East, Whitney again entreated Congress to act. This time he presented them with specific geographical details for a transcontinental route, and offered to build the railroad himself in exchange for a land grant sixty miles wide from Lake Michigan to the Pacific. By selling off this land as the road was being built, Whitney said, he could raise sufficient funds to pay expenses for construction. He estimated that the great work could be accomplished in less than fifteen years, and that 'the over-population of Europe must and will flock to it'.

The main obstacle as he saw it was the occupancy of the Indians, their land titles not having been extinguished, but Whitney assured the Congress that the native Americans were 'ready and willing to sell all that may be desirable for this object, and for a very small sum ... and this road would produce a revolution in the situation of the red as well as the white man. The Sioux Indians occupy and claim nearly all the lands from above latitude of about 43° from the Mississippi to the Rocky Mountains. They are numerous, powerful, and entirely savage.'

Whitney shrewdly pointed out that the building of the railroad would drive the 'savage' Sioux and their buffalo northward, 'and we can then succeed in bringing the removed and small tribes to habits of industry and civilization, and their race may be preserved until mixed and blended with ours, and the Sioux must soon follow them.'

The transcontinental railroad was a part of the nation's destiny, Whitney maintained, a destiny that could not be realized without it. 'Now *only* is the time in which it can be done ... some one's whole efforts, energies, and life must be devoted to it.' And if he, Asa Whitney, could be the instrument to accomplish this great work, that honour would be enough; he would ask no more.

By this time Whitney had aroused the suspicions of the South. That region's commercial interests wanted no part of a transcontinental railroad originating on the shore of Lake Michigan, and their political representatives in Washington began a drumfire of publicity against 'the railroad schemes of Asa Whitney'.

In the late 1840s, largely as the result of the efforts of Whitney and John Plumbe, a series of railroad conventions was held in various cities, every one of which yearned to become the originating point for the first transcontinental railway. At one of these meetings in Chicago in 1847, Whitney's plan was condemned, and during the following months an imposing number of opponents began offering rival proposals. Stephen A. Douglas, who was soon to achieve fame in his debates with Abraham Lincoln, represented the Chicago viewpoint and advocated a route to Council Bluffs that would later be followed by the Chicago & Rock Island Railroad. The arguments offered against Whitney's route were that it was too far to the north; the climate was harsh; there was no fuel for Iron Horses; the Indians were hostile; and the land would probably never be inhabited by white settlers. One opposition group called it 'a scheme of gigantic robbery'.

Another of Whitney's enemies was Senator Thomas Hart Benton of Missouri, a leader in the national movement to acquire more Western territory for the United States. Benton wanted St Louis to be the terminus for the transcontinental route, and quoted his son-in-law, the five-foot-two-inch-tall explorer John C. Frémont, as advocating 'a great central path' along the Santa Fe Trail to Bent's Fort and then through the Rockies at Cochetopa Pass. In one of his speeches Benton visualized an Iron Horse puffing alongside a Rocky Mountain Peak transformed by a sculptor into a giant statue of Columbus, with one arm extended westward, the other holding an inscribed tablet: THERE LIES THE EAST! THERE LIES INDIA! As for Sam Houston of Texas, he of course wanted assurances that the road would pass through that recently annexed state.

35

Among the Southerners who opposed Whitney was John C. Calhoun, who had reached the melancholy conclusion that the South and the North were already acting as two nations. If there was to be a transcontinental railroad, he and his followers wanted the Charleston & Memphis road to be extended westward from the latter city. As for New Orleans, the port city, its leaders bitterly opposed all proposed routes across the continent and fought for a sea-and-land route that would use the narrow isthmus of Panama, or Tehuantepec as it was then called, for a short and inexpensive connecting railroad.

During the lively debates over all these various routes, no mention was ever made of the native Americans, the Indians who had lived for centuries on the lands into which the Iron Horses must intrude, puffing and steaming and trailing dark smoke plumes. The Indians were ignored as completely as if they held no more rights to the land than did the buffalo or the antelope. Only Asa Whitney remembered them, and his principal concern was to extinguish their land titles and then either force them to become like white men or drive them out of the way.

Despite all the opposition to Whitney, in July 1848 he managed to get a bill introduced in the Senate 'to set apart and sell to Asa Whitney, of New York, a portion of the public lands, to enable him to construct a railroad from Lake Michigan to the Pacific Ocean.' Senator Benton immediately led a fierce attack upon the bill and won the support of the majority, who felt that a thorough survey of all possible routes to the Pacific should be undertaken before Congress took further action.

A few months later, with the Mexican War ended and vast land spoils in the West awaiting division between partisans of the North and South, two significant railroad conventions were held in St Louis and Memphis. Hundreds of representatives from all parts of the United States attended, but all they could agree upon was that the US Army should make an extensive series of surveys to determine the best route for a railroad. Asa Whitney attended the conventions, and as he listened to the debates it must have been apparent to him that no compromise on the location of a transcontinental railroad would ever be reached. As John C. Calhoun had already realized, the United States was not one nation but two, and out of the bitter rivalries secession and war were all but inevitable.

In a last desperate attempt to secure financial backing for his railroad to the Western Sea, Whitney journeyed to England in 1851, but he found that the bankers there were involved in other varieties of exploitation. Typical of the attitudes he confronted was this comment by a London newspaper: 'If our friends should really get from the Mississippi to Oregon, it will be a thousand pities that they should stop there. A tubular bridge across Behring's [sic] strait would literally put a girdle round the earth – and then the predilection of American citizens might be gratified by the establishment of a perpetual circulation.'

After seven years of effort, Asa Whitney now abandoned his dream of the Iron Horse and the Western Sea. Retiring to his dairy farm at Locust Hill near Washington, he peddled milk in the nation's capital, enjoying life too much to destroy it by suicide as John Plumbe had done, and although he took no further part in the building of a transcontinental railroad, he did live to see his dream accomplished.

Meanwhile, in its usual ponderous manner, Congress got around to authorizing the Secretary of War, on 1 March 1853, to employ the Corps of Topographical Engineers to make surveys to ascertain the 'most practical and economical route for a railroad from the Mississippi River to the Pacific Ocean'. The Secretary of War was Jefferson Davis, and being a Southern leader he had already settled upon a rail route between the 32nd and 35th parallels. Nevertheless, Davis quickly ordered engineering expeditions into the field to explore possible routes along parallels as far north as the Canadian border. One reason for the Secretary's haste was that Congress had granted him only ten months to complete the surveys, an almost impossible task considering the state of transportation at that time and the difficulties of determining grades and finding suitable passes through the Rocky Mountains.

Throughout its history, the Army Corps of Engineers has had a covert and often corrupt relationship with politicians, and the episode of the Pacific railway surveys was no exception. Soon after the surveys began, a company that called itself the Atlantic

& Pacific Railroad was founded in New York. It proposed to build a transcontinental railroad from a Southern terminus across Texas between the 32nd and 35th parallels to what was then the village of San Diego, California. The president of the Atlantic & Pacific was one Robert J. Walker, a former senator who had been involved in land scandals, bond repudiations, and other high-finance confidence schemes in Mississippi. Jefferson Davis owed a considerable political debt to Walker, whose influence and sponsorship had made possible the rise to power of the future President of the Confederacy.

Furthermore, Walker was the brother-in-law of Major William Helmsley Emory, a haughty red-bearded Maryland aristocrat, a West Point graduate, and one of the most influential officers of the Army's Topographical Engineers. Emory had accompanied General Stephen Watts Kearny's Army of the West on its triumphal conquest of New Mexico and California in 1846, and he and a number of fellow officers had acquired large holdings of real estate for modest sums around the village of San Diego. A transcontinental railroad with a western terminus at San Diego would make them all very rich. Furthermore, the commander of the Corps of Topographical Engineers, Colonel John James Abert of Virginia, was so interested in the Southern route that even before the Pacific railroad surveys were authorized, he sent Lieutenant-Colonel Joseph E. Johnston (later an important Confederate general) to Texas to find a rail route by way of El Paso to San Diego.

Outside the closed orbit of the Corps of Engineers were others with private gains to be promoted. Senator Thomas Hart Benton was so determined that St Louis (which lies between the 38th and 39th parallels) should be the terminus, and he so distrusted the Corps of Engineers, that he dispatched his own surveying party, complete with a press agent, to find a route westward along the 38th parallel. And then Benton's son-in-law, John C. Frémont, followed up with still another survey along the 38th to make certain that the most favourable route would end not in San Diego but in northern California, where Frémont himself claimed sizable land holdings. Another proponent of the St Louis terminus was Pierre Chouteau, who had grown wealthy in the fur trade. As the fur trade was declining, Chouteau put his money into a St Louis factory to make iron rails and went to Washington to lobby for the 38th parallel route.

A former officer of the Corps of Engineers, Isaac Stevens, was equally determined to convince the government that Asa Whitney's long-promoted route between the 47th and 49th parallels was far superior to the others. Not long before the surveys were authorized, the politically inclined Stevens had resigned his commission in the Engineers to become governor of Washington Territory. In this vast and unexploited land he hoped to build his political and economic fortunes, and he needed the transcontinental railroad to ensure fulfillment of his dream. Although he was now a civilian, Stevens persuaded Jefferson Davis to let him direct the military personnel of this Northern survey party. Among the officers was Captain George B. McClellan, later to become commander of the Union Army and a candidate for President of the United States.

Stephen A. Douglas, another ambitious politician, owned enough strategically located land in Chicago to become a millionaire if his favoured route westward through Council Bluffs and Omaha was chosen, but being a shrewd businessman he hedged on his bets by buying up the site of a proposed terminus on Lake Superior after he learned that Isaac Stevens's survey might be shortened to that point. As for Douglas's rival, Abraham Lincoln, the future President evidently agreed with his debating partner that the route through Council Bluffs-Omaha and South Pass was the most practical. Lincoln acquired land interests at Council Bluffs.

Insofar as facilitating the selection of a railroad route across the West, the surveys of the Corps of Engineers accomplished nothing. As the reports were published, Southern partisans exaggerated the advantages of the 32nd parallel and the disadvantages of the 48th. Northern partisans took the opposite position, and in the highly charged atmosphere of the 1850s neither side was willing to accept a compromise route. The government spent more than a million dollars in publishing over a period of five years the thirteen quarto volumes of explorations and surveys for a Pacific railroad, and although they contained little information that would have assisted a field surveyor in marking out a railway line, they were filled with an extraordinary amount of detail relating to geology, geography, land forms, American Indians, weather, trails, botanical specimens, birds, mammals, reptiles, and fish. Hundreds of illustrations, many of them tinted, accompanied the text; an artist was attached to each surveying party, and most of the pictures were drawn in the field. Today, the reports stand not as a guide for the routing of railroads but as a priceless compendium of the virgin West immediately before its despoilation by the Iron Horse.

Surprisingly, the route along which the first transcontinental railway eventually was built was not surveyed by any of the exploring parties of the Corps of Engineers. Its various sections were already well known of course to fur traders, Oregon-bound emigrants, and California goldseekers. It lay between the 40th and 45th parallels, a band across the continent that has long fascinated meteorologists and geographers because it is the track of America's most intense climatic storms, a broad swath of highly charged energy that apparently is transferable to its human inhabitants. The great centres of production in America are within this belt. It is worth noting that several members of the Pacific railroad survey parties compared the routes they were surveying with this well-known South Pass route, and that they usually favoured the latter, which lies directly across the 42nd parallel.

Soon after the railroad survey expeditions were sent into the field, another curiously related series of governmental actions began to take place. In August 1853, the President of the United States, Franklin Pierce, ordered the Commissioner of Indian Affairs, George W. Manypenny, 'to visit the Indian country to confer with the various tribes, as a preliminary measure, looking to negotiation with them for the purpose of procuring their assent to a territorial government and the extinguishment of their title, in whole or in part, to the lands owned by them.'

Manypenny did not visit tribes of the far Southwest or the Northwest; he went nowhere near the parallels favoured for transcontinental railroad routes by partisans of the South or North. Instead, he visited the Omaha, Oto, and Missouri, the Sauk and

Fox, the Kickapoo, Delaware, and Shawnee – mostly tribes that only a few years earlier had been driven across the Mississippi to new lands that they had been promised were theirs 'as long as the grass shall grow or the waters run'. With these tribes Commissioner Manypenny made treaties from 1854 through 1857, taking from the Indians vast areas of land for the government of the United States.

For instance, on 6 May 1854, Manypenny persuaded the Delawares to cede to the United States all their land except eighty acres to be reserved for each tribal allottee, and convinced them that the value of these remaining holdings would be greatly enhanced by a railroad through their country. (Eventually the Delawares were forced to surrender all their land and retreat to Indian territory, where they completely vanished as a tribe.) On 17 May four representatives of the Sauk and Fox tribes were invited to visit Washington, and while there they ceded four hundred square miles of land. When the series of treaties was completed, these Indians had surrendered title to 18 million of their 19,342,000 acres, most of which lay along or was adjacent to the belt bound by the 40th and 45th parallels. Evidently there was some spoken or unspoken consensus within the government that the rail route to the Western Sea would follow the parallels of the lower forties, and so the lands were made ready, titles duly legitimized, for transfer to the exploiters of the first transcontinental railroad.

THREE

War Slows the March to the Western Sea

During the 1840s when Mark Twain was participating in various escapades around Hannibal, Missouri, with his fellow teenager Tom Blankenship (whom he later immortalized as Huckleberry Finn), the town was astir with rumours of a railroad. Hannibal was a riverboat town on the Mississippi and mainly Southern in its attitudes, but railroad fever was everywhere. Anybody who owned a map could see that a railroad running west from Hannibal to the Missouri River would cut several hundred miles off the long haul down to St Louis and then up the Missouri to its big bend where Kansas and Nebraska began. When the town's businessmen gathered to discuss the railroad, they often met in the office of Hannibal's justice of the peace, John Clemens, who was Mark Twain's father.

For their Missouri River terminus, the Hannibal railroad enthusiasts came to favour St Joseph, which had been a prosperous fur-trading post for half a century, and in 1849, after the discovery of gold in California, quickly turned into a boom town. As many as twenty steamboats a day stopped at St Joe to unload hordes of emigrants and goldseekers bound west from there on wagon trains. To supply this migration, food, tools, clothing, wagons, and horses also had to be brought up the river. 'St Joseph is quite a village and doing quite a great deal of business at this time,' one westbound traveller recorded, 'but the way they fleece the California emigrants is worth noticing.'

Hannibal's merchants and bankers had taken notice and were eager to share in this Western money flow. Some envisioned their railroad as pausing only temporarily at St Joseph before bridging the Missouri and plunging on across the continent to the Western Sea. Raising money to build a railroad was a slow process, however, and before the dreams and talk were translated to action John Clemens died, leaving young Samuel (Mark Twain) Clemens an orphan.

Not until the autumn of 1850 did the charter holders of the Hannibal & St Joseph Railroad suddenly discover a way in which they could finance their project. In September of that year, the Congress established a precedent in government aid by granting more than two million acres of public land to the Illinois Central Company to be used in raising money for construction of a railroad from Chicago straight southward to the town of Cairo at the confluence of the Ohio and Mississippi rivers. With this example before them, representatives of the Hannibal & St Joseph hastened to Washington and demanded the same kind of grant – six sections of land for each mile of completed track – and they got it. With millions of dollars worth of Missouri farmland under its control, the Hannibal & St Joseph soon found itself being wooed by financial giants from the East.

Setting another pattern that would be followed in construction of the first transcontinental railroad, the directors of the Hannibal & St Joseph built simultaneously from the eastern and western ends of their survey. In this way, the railroad reached the Missouri River long before any of its rivals. On 13 February 1859, Joseph Robidoux, the old Mountain Man who founded St Joseph for the American Fur Company, drove a golden spike at Cream Ridge near Chillicothe, and the Hannibal & St Joseph was completed. As Rock Island had done exactly five years earlier, the town of St Joe postponed its celebration until Washington's Birthday. To mark the great occasion, a jug of water from the Mississippi was hauled overland by the railroad to St Joe, and there with appropriate oratory the contents were mingled with the waters of the muddy Missouri. In that year, Mark Twain was earning his living as a steersman on a Mississippi River steamboat.

Other events significant to Western railroads occurred during 1859. At about the same time that the first Iron Horse came steaming into St Joe, a young Pennsylvanian who had emigrated westward to seek his fortune was persuading the Kansas territorial legislature to grant him a railroad charter. He was mutton-chop-whiskered Cyrus K. Holliday, one of the founders and the first mayor of the capital city of Topeka. His railroad vision was a track running from the Missouri River to Topeka and then westward along the old Santa Fe Trail – the Atchison, Topeka & Santa Fe. With the help of two powerful senators, Holliday was soon beseeching the federal government for a land grant, but it was 3 March 1863, before President Lincoln signed the act that gave the paper railroad 2,928,928 acres of the people's land in Kansas, and eventually millions more in states farther west.

In August 1859, Abraham Lincoln, whose signature was to make effective three immense railroad grants during his later presidency, was in Council Bluffs, Iowa. He was there to inquire into realty holdings that he had taken as security for a debt and also a homestead allotment due him for militia service in the Black Hawk War. At the hotel where Lincoln was staying he met a sturdy, dark-bearded young man of twenty-eight who had just returned from a journey up the Platte Valley. The young man was Grenville Dodge, and he had been making a preliminary survey along the 42nd parallel for his employer, Henry Farnam of the Rock Island and Mississippi & Missouri railroads. 'We sat down on the bench on the porch of the Pacific House,' Dodge said afterwards, 'and he [Lincoln] proceeded to find out all about the country we had been through, and all about our railroad surveys ... in fact, he extracted from me the information I had gathered for my employers, and virtually shelled my woods most thoroughly.'

Whether Lincoln was impressed by young Dodge's arguments for a Council Bluffs-Omaha terminus for a transcontinental railroad is difficult to determine. In later life Dodge proved himself to be such an accomplished twister of the truth that all his statements must be carefully examined. Years afterwards, Dodge claimed that Lincoln summoned him to a meeting in the White House during the spring of 1863 and that their discussion led to the President's using his authority to designate Council Bluffs as the starting point of the Union Pacific Railroad. The record shows, however, that Dodge was nowhere near Washington in the spring of 1863 and that Lincoln made his decision several months later, after meeting with Thomas Durant and Peter Dey. It is likewise difficult to determine what influence Dodge may have had upon Durant, or what significance there may be in the fact that both

Dodge and Lincoln owned land in the Council Bluffs area.

It was also during 1859 that a thirty-three-year-old Connecticut Yankee devoted his days to persuading assemblymen in Sacramento, capital of the new state of California, that they should take the initiative in building a railroad to the East, from whence most of them had come. He was Theodore Judah, a civil engineer who had journeyed there to help build a short-line railroad from Sacramento to the gold mines east of the town. Before the road was completed, Judah became infected with the same fanaticism that had driven John Plumbe and Asa Whitney in their fruitless efforts to promote a transcontinental railway.

Although his humourless persistence won him the name 'Crazy Judah', he managed to assemble a number of delegates in October 1859 at San Francisco for an official California railroad convention. Representatives of stagecoach and steamboat interests ridiculed Judah's belief that a railroad could be built across the rugged Sierras, but he persuaded the delegates to endorse a route eastward by way of the California overland trail which after passing through the Rockies followed the Platte Valley to Omaha and Council Bluffs. Perhaps as much to be rid of him as to support him, the delegates then voted to send Judah to Washington to lobby for his transcontinental railroad. Unlike his visionary predecessors, Theodore Dehone Judah was a trained engineer and a bulldog; the world would soon hear more of him.

In 1859, however, the Hannibal & St Joseph Railroad seemed to be the most likely candidate for extension across the continent. It was the only completed rail route to the overland staging towns along the Missouri, and its passenger and freight traffic was heavy and profitable. In the spring of the following year, the road's hopes were boosted even more when Pony Express mail service to California was inaugurated at St Joseph.

At about noon on 3 April 1860, a special messenger carrying mail from New York, Washington, and other Eastern cities crossed the Mississippi by ferry and boarded a special train on the Hannibal & St Joseph. That day the engineer set a record that was not beaten for fifty years, by bringing the messenger into St Joe in less than five hours, just in time to transfer the mail to the saddlebags of Johnny Frey, the first Pony Express rider. Flags were flying, bands were playing, and crowds were cheering orators who predicted that the Hannibal & St Joe would soon extend its tracks 'upon which a tireless Iron Horse will start his overland journey'. A cannon boomed and jockey-sized Johnny Frey leaped into his saddle and galloped for the ferry that would take him across the Missouri to begin the long 1,966-mile run to California. 'Hardly will the cloud of dust which envelops the rider die away,' said St Joseph's mayor Jeff Thompson, 'before the puff of steam will be seen upon the horizon.' So certain were the directors of the railroad that they would soon be hauling mail all the way to California, they ordered construction of a post-office car, the first of its kind, upon which mail could be sorted and bagged.

In that summer of 1860, however, the madness of oncoming war was spreading across the nation, and before another year passed, the diminutive Johnny Frey exchanged his Pony Express buckskins for the blue uniform of the Union Army. He marched off towards the South to die at the hands of the Arkansas Rangers. Mayor Jeff Thompson chose the grey uniform of the Confederacy and was soon leading guerrilla cavalry raids against the railroad he had so much praised and admired, the Hannibal & St Joseph. As for Mark Twain, he became an unemployed steamboat pilot when war closed the Mississippi River to commercial steamboat traffic. He returned to pro-Southern Hannibal and drilled briefly with a group of young men he had known since boyhood. They called themselves the Hannibal Confederate Militia, but after a few days they became bored with drilling in the woods and disbanded. Not long afterwards, Mark and his brother Orion (who had campaigned for Abraham Lincoln and been rewarded with a lucrative government appointment in Nevada Territory) arrived in St Joseph. There they boarded a stagecoach bound west for the land of the future, leaving the Civil War behind them.

In the meantime, 'Crazy Ted' Judah, having had little success as a lobbyist for his Pacific railroad, left Washington to return to California. He was still determined to build a transcontinental road. His new plan was to form a railroad company and sell enough stock to public-spirited Californians to get construction started. Being a practical engineer, he knew that he could not extract funds from practical businessmen until he proved to them that Iron Horses could cross the formidable Sierras. Discarding the impractical survey made in 1854 by Lieutenant Edward G. Beckwith for the Corps of Engineers, Judah went into the Sierras and made his own survey. An investor in a railroad, he reasoned, 'does not care to be informed that there are 999 different varieties and species of plants and herbs, or that grass is abundant at that point; or buffalo scarce at that. His inquiries are somewhat more to the point. He wishes to know the length of your road. He says, let me see your map and profile, that I may judge of its alignment and grades ... Have you any tunnels, and what are their circumstances? ... How many bridges, river crossings ... how about timber and fuel? Where is the estimate of the cost of your road, and let me see its detail.'

And so while Civil War battles raged in the East, Judah spent the summer mapping out a route through the Sierras that was more than a hundred miles shorter than the Corps of Engineers' survey. It would run from Dutch Flat through Donner Pass and the Truckee River canyon, and then down to the Washoe gold country of Nevada. It was the recent discovery of gold and silver, the fabulous Comstock Lode, in Nevada that helped more than anything else to attract Sacramento's business leaders to Judah's railroad dream. The California gold rush, which had made them wealthy, was declining, and they were eager to extend their money-making enterprises into Nevada. Judah's railroad might never be completed, but his plan required a wagon road for hauling supplies, and whoever owned that highway would control commerce into and out of the booming Nevada mining towns.

Several of Sacramento's leading merchants, therefore, decided to join 'Crazy Judah' in his railroad scheme. Leland Stanford operated a wholesale grocery business and was planning to run for governor as a candidate of Abraham Lincoln's new political party, the Republicans. Collis P. Huntington and Mark Hopkins had started a miners' supply store in a small tent in Sacramento and had built it into the largest hardware enterprise on the Pacific Coast. Charles Crocker owned a dry-goods store. Others were jewellers, owners of mines, traders of various sorts. But it was Stanford, Huntington, Hopkins, and Crocker – the Big Four – who would dominate the railroad that they incorporated on 28 June

1861, as the Central Pacific Railroad of California. Stanford was president, Huntington vice-president, Hopkins treasurer, and Judah the chief engineer. On 9 October the officers approved Judah's final survey and ordered him to return to Washington as an accredited agent of the Central Pacific 'for the purpose of procuring appropriations of land and US bonds from the government, to aid in the construction of this road.'

Soon after Judah arrived in Washington, the recently completed telegraph line across the continent brought the news that Leland Stanford had been elected governor of California. The chief engineer was delighted, of course; he had not yet discovered that he was involved with men who could be absolutely ruthless wherever money was concerned. He was in somewhat the same position as Henry Farnam, but Farnam had only Dr Durant to contend with while Judah had four men possessed of the same rapacious qualities.

As he was beginning his campaign for government assistance, Judah discovered that other railroad forces were hard at work on Capitol Hill. Representatives of the Hannibal & St Joseph were there, of course, but the most energetic group was headed by James C. Stone, president of the Leavenworth, Pawnee & Western Railroad Company. Stone employed a professional lobbyist to manage his campaign, although the Leavenworth company like the Central Pacific was only a paper railroad. With the assistance of the US Office of Indian Affairs, however, it had swindled the Potawatomies and Delawares out of exclusive rights to hundreds of thousands of acres of tribal land.

In reporting this transaction from Leavenworth, Indian agent Thomas B. Sykes described the land as 'surplus' and valued it at $1.25 per acre, although similar land in the area was then selling for ten dollars per acre. 'By this treaty fifty miles of railroad is secured to the Territory of Kansas, without one dollar being paid from the territorial treasury or by the general government ... This is the first and greatest link in the great Pacific railway, west of the State of Missouri. It is another step toward the Pacific shores. It is another link in the iron chain that is to bind the Atlantic to the Pacific.'

Agent Sykes failed to mention that not one foot of track had yet been laid, nor did this fact seem to concern the Leavenworth lobbyists in Washington. They had a good supply of stock certificates and land titles, which they showered upon influential Washingtonians such as Senator J. F. Simmons, journalist Benjamin Perley Poore, and politicians Thaddeus Stevens and James G. Blaine. Chief engineer Judah of the Central Pacific soon found himself working in close alliance with the Leavenworth promoters, and duly received twelve hundred shares of Leavenworth stock. During the spring of 1862, while armies were locked in battle in nearby Virginia, Thomas Durant joined the lobbyists. His aim of course was to persuade Congress to designate a transcontinental route across Nebraska from Omaha-Council Bluffs, but he appeared willing to compromise provided that there was money in it for him. Not long afterwards, Collis Huntington, the domineering, heavy-framed vice-president of the Central Pacific, arrived in Washington. Evidently he feared that chief engineer Judah was not aggressive enough to make certain that Congress would give the Central Pacific everything it wanted.

Had the Civil War not been in progress, the powerful lobby of the Leavenworth group and the demonstrated success of the Hannibal & St Joe Railroad quite likely would have swung Congress to their choice as the first links in a transcontinental railroad. Unfortunately for these companies, however, the Confederates were raising hell with Missouri railroads, wrecking trains, blowing up bridges, and capturing trainmen. The Rebels went so far as to kidnap the president of the Hannibal & St Joe, threatening to shoot him unless he ordered train service completely halted. As for the projected Leavenworth railroad, it also was in border territory, vulnerable to raids by William Quantrill, Sterling Price, and other Confederate cavalry leaders.

It was soon obvious to those preparing the 'Act to Aid in the Construction of a Railroad and Telegraph Line from the Missouri River to the Pacific Ocean' that the road would have to be built farther north. In the act's final version, the railroad was given a name, Union Pacific Railroad Company, and it was authorized to construct 'a single line of railroad and telegraph from a point on the western boundary of the State of Iowa to be fixed by the President of the United States.' Upon completion of forty consecutive

49

miles of any part of the railroad, the company would receive title to five alternate sections of land on each side of the line and 'bonds of the United States of one thousand dollars each, payable in thirty years after date, bearing six per centum per annum interest ... to the amount of sixteen said bonds per mile.' In the same act, the Central Pacific was authorized to construct a railroad from the Pacific coast to the eastern boundary of California upon the same terms and conditions as the Union Pacific – which meant that both would receive enormous land grants.

To ease the disappointment of supporters of the Leavenworth, Pawnee & Western and the Hannibal & St Joe, the act also offered generous grants to them, provided that they extended their tracks westward across Kansas and joined the main line of the Union Pacific at the 100th meridian. Then, almost as an afterthought, the authors of the act stated that the government 'shall extinguish as rapidly as may be the Indian titles to all lands falling under the operation of this act', although they made no recommendation as to how this was to be accomplished. In recognition of the difficulties of building a railroad under wartime conditions, the Union Pacific Company was given until 1 July 1876, the centennial of the republic, to lay its tracks to the western boundary of Nevada Territory.

On 1 July 1862, the day that his Army of the Potomac began retreating in Virginia after the Battle of Malvern Hill, President Lincoln signed the act, creating the Union Pacific Railroad Company. Thus was assured the fortunes of a dynasty of American families, many of whose names appear in the documents as 'commissioners', 158 of them – Brewsters, Bushells, Olcotts, Harkers, Harrisons, Trowbridges, Langworthys, Reids, Ogdens, Bradfords, Noyeses, Brooks, Cornells, and dozens of others, including Huntington and Judah and a handful of swaggering frontier buccaneers such as Ben Holladay, the stagecoach king of the West.

Huntington and Judah wasted no time in transferring their company's activities to New York, where they established credit and placed orders for rails and locomotives for shipment by sea to California. Competition for any sort of iron was intense because of wartime demands for guns and military rolling stock. They were also handicapped by a restrictive clause in the Union Pacific act, which had been added by that wily old congressman from Pennsylvania, Thaddeus Stevens. Although Stevens had received a block of Leavenworth stock in exchange for his vote, that was not sufficient to satisfy him. He had also demanded insertion of a clause requiring that 'all iron used in the construction and equipment of said road to be American manufacture'. In addition to being a congressman, Stevens was an iron manufacturer. Consequently, when Huntington and Judah found themselves faced with high prices and long delays in obtaining rails and other equipment, they were forbidden to buy British iron, which was readily available and comparatively inexpensive and could have been delivered by sea to California almost as quickly as from New York.

In spite of these difficulties, the energetic founders of the Central Pacific managed to assemble enough equipment in California by the end of the year to announce that ground-breaking ceremonies would be held in Sacramento on 8 January 1863. On that morning heavy rains muddied the streets, but before noon the sun was shining brightly and a procession of carriages decorated in patriotic bunting wound hub-deep through the mud to a temporary platform near the Front Street levee a short distance above K Street. Bales of hay had to be strewn around the platform so that spectators would not sink into the mire while listening to the oratory. Even then, most of the women refused to subject their long skirts to the muck and so made their way to the balcony of a nearby hotel where a local brass band had also taken refuge.

The ceremonies began with the band playing 'Wait for the Wagon' while two flag-covered wagons rolled up before the rostrum. On one of them was a large banner depicting hands clasped across the continent and bearing an inscription: MAY THE BOND BE ETERNAL.

After an interminable invocation by the local minister, Charlie Crocker, the former dry-goods merchant who now called himself general superintendent of the Central Pacific Railroad, arose to start the speech-making. Crocker's face was deeply flushed above his chin beard; he weighed more than 250 pounds and could bellow like a bull. At high noon he introduced the president of the Central Pacific, who was also the governor of California, Leland

Stanford. Dignified in his frock coat and high silk hat, Stanford promised that the Pacific and Atlantic coasts would soon be bound by iron bonds. On the agenda of the day, his next duty was to turn the first spadeful of earth that would start construction of the railroad. As this was an impossible feat to accomplish in the straw-covered mud, someone had thoughtfully loaded a tubful of dry dirt into one of the wagons, and Stanford gravely leaned from the platform and lifted out a spadeful. 'Nine cheers!' shouted Charlie Crocker, and the crowd responded.

'Everybody felt happy,' reported the *Sacramento Union*, 'because after so many years of dreaming, scheming, talking and toiling, they saw with their own eyes the actual commencement of a Pacific railroad.' Ironically, the man whose dreams and schemes had led to this happy celebration was not present on that day. He was in the East, on one of his periodic journeys by sea and isthmus, desperately trying to obtain enough credit and iron to get the railroad built. A few months later, as he was crossing through the Panama jungles, a mosquito bit him, and on 2 November 1863, Theodore Judah died of yellow fever. Now his railroad was completely in the hands of greedy exploiters – the Big Four – Stanford, Huntington, Crocker, and Hopkins.

Meanwhile in the East, the Union Pacific Railroad was off to a much slower start. The bitter Civil War was closer at hand (the orators in faraway Sacramento had scarcely mentioned that conflict). In addition, the Union Pacific's ownership was much more numerous and diffused than that of the Central Pacific. Several ambitious men were jockeying for control, but none had been successful. In September 1862, sixty-eight of the original 'commissioners' assembled in Chicago to hold their first meeting. They passed various resolutions, recommended the opening of stock subscription books in all the principal cities of the Union, and assured one another that 'the pressure of war should not discourage the friends of the work, nor deter them from entering vigorously upon its prosecution.' About all that was accomplished was the election of William B. Ogden of Chicago as president and Henry V. Poor as secretary. Ogden was already well on the way towards establishing his family's fortune through railroad promotion, and Poor was editor of the *Railroad Journal* and an avid collector of statistics on the subject.

Although Dr Thomas Durant was not one of the Union Pacific commissioners and did not attend the original meeting in Chicago, he spent a considerable amount of his time during 1863 in scheming to seize the seat of power in that yet amorphous organization. According to the act that created the transcontinental railroad, two million dollars in stock had to be sold before construction could begin, and no one person could subscribe to more than two hundred shares at a thousand dollars per share, ten per cent down. Noting that stock sales were moving very slowly (only 150 shares had been subscribed by March 1863), Durant adroitly arranged to buy more than the required two million dollars in stock in the names of several friends. Dr Durant himself paid the ten per cent down payment for them. Not only was he now in a position to control the next election of officers, which was set for October 1863, he was also ready to unload some of his Mississippi & Missouri stock at a profit sufficient to recover the down payments he had made for his friends on the Union Pacific stock. Although construction of the Mississippi & Missouri Railroad was still stalled in the middle of Iowa, Durant slyly released stories to the press announcing that the M & M Railroad had been 'selected as the commencement of the Pacific route'. As usual, Durant's trick worked. The stock soared in price and he sold out at the high point, increasing his personal fortunes considerably.

And then on 30 October at the organizational meeting of the Union Pacific in New York, Durant, using his majority of stockholder votes, replaced Ogden as president with old John A. Dix, the powerful politician who had worked to secure the Iowa land grants for Durant's M. & M. Dix was an excellent choice to serve as front man for Durant. He had a reputation for honesty, and spent most of his time strutting about Washington in a general's uniform. Durant knew that Dix would never bother him. Henry Poor, the railroad statistician, remained as secretary. As for Durant himself, he chose the title 'vice-president and general manager', and he was so elected.

During this period of intense manipulation, a new associate had moved into Dr Durant's orbit. He was George Francis Train, an unpredictable eccentric who had made a fortune in shipping and railroads. Train had been dabbling in street railways in England when the Civil War brought him back to America to help save the

Union. He was still in his early thirties, and when chance brought him in touch with Durant, the romance of the transcontinental railroad immediately aroused his enthusiasm. In their viewpoints, Train and Durant were opposites. Durant enjoyed the acquisition of money and he had the patience of a spider in weaving webs to snare it. Train had little regard for money other than to use it in the enjoyment of life; his zest for action kept him in a state of perpetual impatience.

Train could not understand why the Union Pacific was so slow in getting construction started at Omaha. After all, almost a year had passed since the Central Pacific had broken ground at Sacramento, and its contractors were already laying track towards the Sierras. Shadows of competition were also on the horizon. President Lincoln had awarded an enormous land grant to Cyrus K. Holliday, and if the Atchison, Topeka & Santa Fe started moving it might well win support for a transcontinental route from a changeable Congress. An even greater threat appeared in the person of John C. Frémont. His father-in-law, Thomas Hart Benton, had died in 1858, but their old dream of a route from St Louis along the 38th parallel still persisted in Frémont's mind. Frémont had made a fortune from gold discovered on his California holdings. In 1863 he used a good part of it to form a partnership with Samuel Hallett and buy a controlling interest in the Leavenworth, Pawnee & Western. At Frémont's insistence, they changed the name to Union Pacific Railway, Eastern Division. Frémont meant to take his railroad to the Western Sea. In the summer of 1863, while Union armies were winning great victories at Gettysburg and Vicksburg, he advertised for four thousand tons of iron rails to be delivered at Leavenworth.

The impatient George Francis Train therefore had little difficulty in persuading Durant that the Union Pacific must hold a ground-breaking ceremony at Omaha. On 2 December 1863, two miles south of the ferry landing at Council Bluffs, several hundred people including the governor of Nebraska and two companies of artillery assembled to hear Train deliver one of his impassioned orations. 'The great Pacific railway is commenced,' he cried, 'at the entrance of a garden 700 miles in length and twenty broad. The Pacific railroad is the nation and the nation is the Pacific railway. This is the grandest enterprise under God!'

In response to a telegram from Durant, engineer Peter Dey, who had run surveys for the westward-pointed railways across Illinois and Iowa, came over from Iowa City. After the governor had turned a spadeful of earth, Dey read messages from Durant and from President Lincoln, the crowd cheered and the artillery companies fired salutes to the great occasion.

Train returned to New York, certain that the railroad would be under construction by spring. A few weeks later, Dey received a telegram informing him that he had been appointed chief engineer of the Union Pacific. As soon as the Nebraska mud dried out in the spring, Dey assembled a small gang of workmen and graded a few miles straight westward from Omaha. In 1864, however, the war was going badly for the Union, the armies suffering their last great bloodbaths before the end. Durant shut down on expenditures and went off to Washington to lobby for increased benefits for the Union Pacific. Train stormed about, impatient at the delay. He visited Omaha from time to time, built a new hotel because he did not like the one that was there, and then casually bought some cheap Omaha real estate, which like everything else he touched rapidly turned into millions of dollars.

At last the war ended, and hordes of young soldiers found themselves cut loose in a changed America. Thousands of them were immigrants – Irish, Germans, Swedes; thousands were former slaves, wandering westward in their first odyssey of freedom; thousands were defeated Confederates whose homes had vanished in the cataclysm of war. They were sturdy, muscular young men accustomed to hardships and dangers, accustomed to taking orders.

Instead of sinking into a slow period of recuperation at the close of its bloodiest war, the nation seemed to pause only momentarily, much like a person taking a deep breath of relief, and then it plunged into a frenetic race to rebuild. The Americans were searching for something – riches and power, riches and greatness, riches and fame. Greed was in the air. The Gilded Age was beginning.

Late in 1865, only a few months after the war's end, steamboats as numerous as wild geese were pushing up the Missouri River towards Omaha. (The railroads in Iowa were still months away from reaching the Missouri.) Some of the boats were loaded with iron rails, locomotives, shovels, ploughs, spikes; others carried passengers, mostly young men heading westward, looking for work. They were all coming together at Omaha, turning the languid trading posts and grog shops into a boom town, a city that would be the nation's centre until parallel rails of iron stretched across the continent.

FOUR

Drill, Ye Tarriers, Drill, While the Owners Take the Plunder

In the late autumn of 1864, while General William Tecumseh Sherman was marching through Georgia and the Civil War seemed close to its end, a dandified Easterner arrived in Omaha to inspect the twenty-three miles of grading that had been completed by chief engineer Peter Dey. His name was Colonel Silas Seymour, and he wore fancy clothing, kept his close-clipped greying hair and goatee neatly brushed at all times, and contrived an aristocratic air. He informed Dey that Dr Durant had appointed him 'consulting engineer' of the Union Pacific and that he was ready to perform his duties.

As the honest Mr Dey was soon to discover, Colonel Seymour's title was a cover for espionage. Durant distrusted Dey, who liked to believe that the managers of the railroad were 'trustees of the bounty of Congress'. Dey also claimed to admire men of 'integrity, purity and singleness of purpose'. The earnest engineer was too much like Henry Farnam to suit Durant's tastes; in fact, Dey made no secret of his wish to have Farnam serve as president of the Union Pacific.

During 1864, Durant had successfully accomplished two major manoeuvres that made it possible for him and his close associates to enter upon a colossal looting of the people's treasury and plundering of national land resources, and he wanted no interference with his plans. The first objective he achieved was establishment of an organization known as the Credit Mobilier. In conversations with George Francis Train, Durant had discussed the practicalities of railroad building and ownership. From previous experience, both men knew that the big money was made by construction contractors rather than by the operators or stockholders. Train recalled a financial organization he had encountered in France – the Société Générale de Crédit Mobilier, which operated as a holding company to siphon off profits from construction of public works. By using such an apparatus, Durant could make contracts with himself at any price per mile he chose to set for construction of the railroad across the continent. Acting as an agent for Durant, Train purchased the charter of an incorporated Pennsylvania fiscal agency and converted it to the Credit Mobilier of America. Durant admitted afterwards that he had gained control of this super-money-making device for a personal expenditure of only five hundred dollars.

Durant's second triumph of the year was to secure passage of a more generous Pacific Railway Act, one that granted twice as much land per mile (12,800 acres instead of 6,400), gave all iron and coal deposits under the land to the railroad, and permitted it to sell first-mortgage bonds to the public. In this grand steal he had the help of that equally greedy lobbyist for the Central Pacific, Collis Huntington. Durant took $437,000 of Union Pacific funds to Washington for lobbying expenses, and although some of his associates later charged that he put most of the money in his own pocket, proof was found that he had spent $18,000 entertaining congressmen at Willard's Hotel. He also spent a great deal more than that distributing Union Pacific stock to congressmen in exchange for their votes. Even by present-day standards of governmental venality, the methods used by Durant and Huntington were exceptionally crude. Congressman Oakes Ames, who with his brother Oliver manufactured shovels in Massachusetts, became a loyal ally and helped to pressure the 1864 Pacific Railway Act through the war-corrupted Congress. The Union Pacific was thus guaranteed a magnificent land grant, 19,000 square miles, a domain larger than the states of Massachusetts, Rhode Island, and Vermont combined. In recognition of their services, Durant invited Oakes and Oliver Ames into the tight little circle of Credit Mobilier stockholders.

With all these arranged riches awaiting the taking, Durant was now ready to begin railroad construction, and his first move was to send one of his New York henchmen to Omaha to sound out Peter Dey. The chief engineer had already submitted estimates of construction costs per mile for the first hundred miles across the rolling prairie country of eastern Nebraska. Dey's estimates averaged between $20,000 and $30,000 per mile, and Durant knew that Dey's figures were close to the real costs. What Durant wanted was an inflated estimate, at least $50,000, which would pour $20,000 to $30,000 per mile of excess profits into the closely held Credit Mobilier. Durant therefore sent one of his couriers, John E. Henry, out to see Dey, and Henry informed the engineer that Durant wanted the estimate raised to $50,000 per mile. As Dey had no knowledge then of the Credit Mobilier scheme, he complied with the request but at the same time made it clear that he believed $30,000 per mile was sufficient to cover costs.

Durant's next move was to arrange for an accomplice named Herbert M. Hoxie to submit a contract bid for construction of the first one hundred miles of railroad at $50,000 per mile. Hoxie was a crafty Iowa politician who had arranged various deals for Durant during the building of the Mississippi & Missouri Railroad in that state. Not long after Durant accepted Hoxie's bid, Hoxie transferred his contract to Credit Mobilier, which was controlled of course by Durant. Later investigations indicated that for this simple piece of paperwork Hoxie received $10,000 in Union Pacific bonds.

In November, Dey received a copy of the transferred Hoxie contract, and immediately suspected Durant's scheme. When Colonel Seymour arrived with the announcement that he was the Union Pacific's 'consulting engineer' and began suggesting changes in the surveyed route westward from Omaha, Dey bluntly refused to cooperate. With Durant's secret backing, however, Seymour then proposed a more circuitous route, one that would require nine more miles of track to reach the same point that Dey's twenty-three miles of preliminary grading reached in a direct line. Seymour's purpose was obvious to Dey: the circuitous route would provide an increased government subsidy during the first days of construction, would enable the Union Pacific to acquire more valuable land close to the developing city of Omaha, and would eliminate a few embankments and bridges. Being an engineer who believed that railroad routes should be shortened wherever possible, Dey could not accept Seymour's proposal for professional reasons. And being an honest man, neither could he accept the inflated Hoxie-Credit Mobilier contract. On 8 December, he wrote his letter of resignation: 'My reasons for this step are simply that I do not approve of the contract made with Mr Hoxie for building the first hundred miles from Omaha west, and I do not care to have my name so connected with the railroad that I shall appear to indorse this contract.'

Durant never bothered to acknowledge Dey's letter of resignation. He simply informed Colonel Seymour that he was now the acting chief engineer of the Union Pacific and should get on with building the circuitous route. (Forty years later, when the UP entered upon a programme of shortening its lines out of Omaha, it abandoned Seymour's route and used Dey's original direct route.) Although Seymour had some experience as a consulting engineer for Eastern railroads, he actually knew very little about railroad construction; for instance, he still believed that parallel timbers made better supports for rails than did cross ties. When he was ordered to use cross ties, he bought cheap cottonwood ties instead of contracting for hardwood, and then after discovering that they rotted quickly he invested hundreds of thousands of dollars in a wood-preservation device. A steam-pressure process known as Burnetizing forced zinc into the cottonwood, but time eventually proved it to be almost worthless.

Samuel B. Reed, who had worked with Dey and Farnam on the railroads out of Chicago, directed most of the surveying for the revised route, and he quickly recognized Seymour for the popinjay he was. Even the Pawnee Indians laughed at Seymour when he rode out on horseback to inspect the progress of the road; on these occasions he usually wore a black silk top hat and carried an umbrella to protect himself from the summer sun.

It was 10 July 1865, before Seymour's crew laid the first rail, and the best they could do across the level prairie was one mile of track per week. In October, when Durant visited Omaha with General William T. Sherman to try to speed up construction, only fifteen miles of track had been completed. Funds were running short, and more miles of track were needed in order to claim more money from the government. The invitation to Sherman was probably one of George Francis Train's promotion ideas, and Durant entered into it enthusiastically. Next to General

Grant, Sherman received more attention from the press than did any other of the Civil War heroes, and the Union Pacific was in dire need of good publicity to spur sales of its stock.

To please Sherman they painted the general's name in gilt letters on Union Pacific Locomotive No 1. As no passenger cars had yet been brought up the Missouri, they attached to the Iron Horse a platform car covered with upended nail kegs to which boards were fastened for seats. Sherman, Durant, Train, and the dozen or so other men in the party wrapped themselves in buffalo robes and rode the fifteen miles to end of track at Sailing's Grove, where they picnicked on roast duck and champagne. 'The party was jolly in going out and hilarious in coming in,' an Omaha newspaper reported. 'Everybody was anxious for a speech from Sherman.'

Sherman made no speech, but between drinks he told of how he had invested money in a proposed railroad while he was stationed in California before the war, and had lost all of his investment. 'I might live to see the day,' he said, 'but can scarcely expect it at my age, when the two oceans will be connected by a complete Pacific railroad.' As Sherman was only forty-five, he undoubtedly was taunting Durant and his associates for their slowness in building tracks across the easily spanned Nebraska plain. During that autumn, some Eastern newspapers had been even more critical, for instance the *New York Times*:

'With numerous plans and many subsidies from Congress, the parties who have been urging the project of a Pacific railroad have failed to carry them out. Their schemes are all broken to pieces, or they are used for speculative purposes, in bolstering up some sinking or perhaps bogus stock ... The people on the Pacific side, with their usual energy, commenced their end of the route some two years since, and, notwithstanding the war and the high price of gold, have ascended over half way from Sacramento City to the summit of the Sierra Nevada mountains.'

Before Sherman departed Omaha, there must have been private conversations about this problem of slackness. Durant was becoming increasingly aware of a provision in the Pacific Railway Act that might cause the Union Pacific to lose its transcontinental subsidy entirely if one of the Kansas railroads should reach the 100th meridian first. That autumn, the old Leavenworth road, which had changed its name to Union Pacific, Eastern Division, completed sixty miles and its work crews were reported to be laying a mile of track each day. Durant made an effort to neutralize the Eastern Division through financial control from New York, but he failed in this and he knew that if the Kansas railroad reached the 100th meridian before the Union Pacific, the government might very well assign it the right to continue building to California.

It was soon obvious to Durant that although Colonel Seymour might be a loyal crony, he lacked the drive to win the now-developing 257-mile race to the 100th meridian. A new chief engineer had to be found, and Sherman highly recommended thirty-five-year-old Grenville Dodge, who had been one of his most dependable generals during the Georgia campaign. Durant remembered Dodge from his work in Illinois and Iowa before the war and was wary of him because of his former close association with Henry Farnam and Peter Dey. Yet he chose Dodge eventually, the young general agreeing to leave the Indian-fighting Army and report for duty in May 1866.

In the meantime, Durant also employed another former general, John S. Casement, who had commanded a division and was from Sherman's home state of Ohio. Before the war Casement had been a track hand in Michigan and then foreman of a track-building gang in Ohio. In the spring of 1866, after accepting the Union Pacific track-laying contract through Durant's Credit Mobilier, Jack Casement and his brother Daniel arrived in Omaha. Standing in his laced boots, Jack Casement reached only five feet four inches, and Dan even shorter, 'five feet nothing'. They resembled a pair of bearded midgets, but those who might have been deceived by their appearance soon joined in the general opinion that they were 'the biggest little men you ever saw'. Adam Schoup, employed by Jack Casement as his personal wagoner, said he 'never saw a man you worked harder for. Many times we drove twenty-four hours, changing horses, and when I played out, Jack drove.'

From the swarms of westward-bound men coming up the Missouri, the Casements hired about a thousand of the sturdiest.

Although tradition holds that most of these men were Irish, there was a goodly number of American-born veterans of the Union and Confederate armies and several former Negro slaves. To fill out the ranks, General Dodge made the startling proposal that the contractors use captured Indians to do the grading, with the Army furnishing 'a guard to make the Indians work, & to keep them from running away'. He was not taken up on this proposition to enslave red men; after all, most of the workers building the railroad had just finished four years of fighting a war to free four million black slaves.

To solve the problem of logistics in building a railroad supplied by a single track pushing out across hundreds of miles of uninhabited country, the Casement brothers invented the 'work train'. To an Iron Horse they attached about a dozen cars, each one designed to serve a special purpose – a car filled with tools, one outfitted as a blacksmith shop, another with rough dining tables and kitchen and commissary, others with built-in bunks, and at the end several flatcars loaded with rails, spikes, fishplates, bolts, and other road-building supplies. It was in fact a self-sufficient small town on wheels.

With the arrival of General Dodge in May, the building of the Union Pacific took on all the aspects of a military operation. 'The men who go ahead [surveyors and locators] are the advance guard,' noted one newspaper correspondent, 'and following them is the second line [the graders] cutting through the gorges, grading the road and building the bridges. Then comes the main body of the army, placing the ties, laying the track, spiking down the rails, perfecting the alignment, ballasting and dressing up and completing the road for immediate use. Along the line of the completed road are construction trains pushing "to the front" with supplies. The advance limit of the rails is occupied by a train of long box-cars with bunks built within them, in which the men sleep at night and take their meals. Close behind this train come train loads of ties, rails, spikes, etc., which are thrown off to the side. A light car drawn by a single horse gallops up, is loaded with this material and then is off again to the front. Two men grasp the forward end of the rail and start ahead with it, the rest of the gang taking hold two by two, until it is clear of the car. At the word of command it is dropped into place, right side up, during which a similar operation has been going on with the rail from the other side – thirty seconds to the rail for each gang, four rails to the minute. As soon as a car is unloaded, it is tipped over to permit another to pass it to the front and then it is righted again and hustled back for another load.

'Close behind the track-layers comes the gaugers, then the spikers and bolters. Three strokes to the spike, ten spikes to the rail, four hundred rails to the mile. Quick work, you say – but the fellows on the Union Pacific are tremendously in earnest.'

Jack and Dan Casement certainly were in earnest. They set a goal of one mile of track per day, offering each track layer a pound of tobacco if a mile of track was laid between sunup and sundown. When they reached that goal, the Casements offered three dollars per day instead of the regular two dollars if the men could lay a mile and a half. And then as the workmen sweated under the midsummer sun, the Casements offered four dollars for two miles a day.

It was at about this time that the iron-men laying the rails, the head spikers, the fishplate bolters, the track liners, and the back-iron men began to sing as they worked. Among the popular songs were 'Whoops Along, Luiza Jane', 'Pat Maloy', and 'Brinon on the Moor'. Off duty, they had harmonicas and jew's harps to accompany their voices, and one workman afterwards recalled singing such gems as 'How Are You Horace Greeley, Does Your Mother Know You're Out?' and 'I'm a Rambling Rake of Poverty, the Son of a Gambolier'.

Exactly when they created their own railroad worksongs is difficult to determine. A contemporary observer noted the peculiar rhythm of track laying, with the track boss commanding 'Down', 'Down', every thirty seconds to signal the dropping of the rails into place. 'They were the pendulum beats of a mighty era; they marked the time of the march and its regulation step.' The spike drivers also developed a grunting exhalation of breath to accompany the rhythmic ring of their sledgehammers, but the railroad ballads of the period seem ill fitted to this beat: 'The great Pacific railway for California hail, Bring on the locomotive, lay down the iron rail', or 'Poor Paddy he works on the railroad'.

More suited was 'Drill, my Paddies, drill. Drill all day, No sugar in your tay, Workin' on the UP Railway'. Not until twenty years later, however, was the chorus of that song – which is more closely associated with the building of the Union Pacific than is any other – set to music and published:

Drill, ye tarriers, drill.
Drill, ye tarriers, drill,
Oh, it's work all day
No sugar in your tay,
Workin' on the U. Pay Ra-ailway!

As for Dr Durant and his cronies, there is no record of what they sang as they collected the $16,000 per mile from the government for the track laid by the workmen, the $25,000 per mile of excess profits from Credit Mobilier, the 12,800 acres of land per mile, and whatever else they were able to divert from the sales of stocks and bonds. Instead of singing, they were always spending money to generate money, and there never seemed to be enough.

By 1 August, the work train was 150 miles west of Omaha, and more labourers were added to the payroll. As the nights grew colder, Casement supplied the men with tents, and every night the tent city moved another mile or two across the plains of Nebraska.

Early in that summer of 1866, the employers of the Casement brothers were given another incentive to loosen their purse strings and speed construction. Congress unexpectedly lifted the Pacific Railway Act's restriction on the Central Pacific, which forbade that railroad to build any farther than 150 miles east of the California-Nevada border. From now on, the meeting point of the two railroads would be determined by the rapidity with which each could lay tracks eastward and westward. The news came like a pistol shot signalling the start of a race across the continent. The Union Pacific responded by employing more graders and throwing them fifty to a hundred miles out ahead of the track layers. General Dodge packed his surveying instruments and with Sam Reed, who had been appointed superintendent of construction, headed for Wyoming to choose the final route through the Rockies.

After the Casement brothers easily won the 247-mile race to the 100th meridian on 5 October 1866, Durant, Train, and Seymour organized a grand excursion to that point on the Nebraska plain. They sent invitations to President Andrew Johnson and members of his cabinet, to all members of Congress and foreign ambassadors, and, more importantly from Durant's viewpoint, to numerous wealthy investors. 'No railroad excursion of similar character and magnitude,' boasted Colonel Seymour, 'had ever been projected in this or any other country.'

President Johnson did not accept; he was growing suspicious of what he called 'the railroad aristocracy' and feared that its financial and political power was replacing the old slave-holding 'oligarchy'. By the time the various parties from the East joined at Omaha, however, the excursionists numbered more than two hundred of the nation's richest and most powerful men and women, with a corps of newspapermen and a photographer to record the events. Being a gourmet himself, Colonel Seymour arranged for elaborate bills of fare to accompany the receptions and balls at Omaha – boiled trout à la Normande, leg of mutton with caper sauce, quails on toast, buffalo tongue, escalloped oysters Louisiana style, antelope with sauce Bigarde, brazed bear in port wine sauce, grouse in Madeira sauce, and teal ducks à la royale.

For the rail journey from Omaha to the 100th meridian, the excursionists boarded four brand-new passenger coaches, and had the run of a saloon car outfitted with a bar, a mess car for meals, the UP directors' car, and Dr Durant's private car, which had been Abraham Lincoln's official car during the war and had been acquired by Durant after it was used to transport the assassinated President's body from Washington to Springfield, Illinois. (The Lincoln car was said to have built inside its walls sheets of boiler plate strong enough to stop rifle bullets. After Durant exchanged it for one of George Pullman's special cars, his associates continued to use the Lincoln car when travelling across the plains where defiant Indians occasionally fired on passing trains. In its later years the ornate fittings were removed, crude wooden seats installed, and it was used to transport immigrants at bargain rates.)

At Columbus, Nebraska, they stopped for the night at a tent

encampment luxuriously furnished with mattresses, buffalo robes, and blankets, and by the light of campfires and a harvest moon they watched a band of Pawnees perform a war dance. The next morning, the train rolled on to the fifteen-hundred-foot Loup-Fork bridge, where the Pawnees, mounted on horses, again entertained with a mock battle. After it was over, Dr Durant paid off the actors with the usual baubles and gimcracks, a gesture meant to please his guests who were unaware that the Pawnees had forced Durant to pay a hundred dollars cash down before they would perform. The Pawnees had been dealing with white men going West for a long time, and had learned the emptiness of their promises and the value of their money.

When the excursionists reached the 100th meridian, instead of finding track layers at work, there was only a wide arched sign bearing the inscription: 100TH MERIDIAN, 247 MILES FROM OMAHA. The Casement brothers and their 'tarriers' had moved on another twenty-two miles west. Eager to show his guests how a railroad was built, Durant ordered the excursion continued to end of track, where they watched the sweating workmen until sundown. Only once did the men pause in their exertions, and that was to pose for a photograph made by Professor John Carbutt, the official *viewist*. At dusk the workmen retired to their crude tent camp to dine on beans and fatback while the excursionists gathered in their luxurious encampment to enjoy lamb with green peas, roasted antelope, and Chinese duck, all washed down with champagne. After dinner Colonel Seymour brought out a case of fireworks, sending up rockets, exploding stars, and pinwheels to keep boredom away until bedtime. Those track builders who were not too weary to stay awake could, of course, share in this heavenly spectacle.

On the return trip the next morning, the train halted beside the 100th meridian arch, and for an hour the dignitaries and their wives posed in various groupings for the official photographer. In one of the prints that has survived, Dr Durant can be seen in a hunting costume, a rifle thrown nonchalantly across his shoulder as he leans against one of the arch supports. Standing slightly apart from him are five other directors of the Union Pacific in long-tailed coats and black silk hats. Behind them is the balloon-stacked Iron Horse decorated with large flags and elkhorns, its tender heaped high with lengths of cottonwood.

Late that evening they were back in Omaha, and as Colonel Seymour reported in his best booster style, 'thus ended the most important and successful celebration of the kind that has ever been attempted in the world.' From his viewpoint and that of the other directors of the UP, the excursion did prove to be a profitable investment. After the return of the politicians and financiers to the East, the attention of the nation was soon fastened upon the activities of the Union Pacific, and millions of dollars in bonds were quickly sold. Many important newspapers began sending correspondents out to the Great Plains, and most of these journalists were treated like visiting royalty by the railroad's representatives. Virtually every report sent back to be published depicted the Union Pacific as a *national* endeavour, a heroic undertaking by the people of America, with the Plains Indians cast in the role of villains. No matter that the Iron Horse was invading traditional hunting grounds of a dozen native tribes, frightening away their food supply of wild game, and tracking across land held sacred for generations – if the 'redskins' resisted, they were evil, because they stood in the way of the compulsive drive towards the Western Sea. In this atmosphere of noble purpose, it became a patriotic duty to invest one's money in Union Pacific stock (even though Credit Mobilier was siphoning off most of the profits) and to defend the transcontinental railroad against subversive detractors, who might have pointed out that although the people of America were paying for the railroad it did not belong to them.

Late in November, with the blizzard season imminent on the plains, the Casement brothers ordered their men into winter quarters at the confluence of the North and South Platte rivers. They named the place North Platte; it was 290 miles west of Omaha. When the construction crew of more than two thousand men erected their tent city, the only permanent structure was the railroad station. But because North Platte was the end of track, it immediately became the staging point for overland traffic to the West. Mormon emigrants bound for Utah gathered in canvas shelters awaiting the spring; soldiers, goldseekers, and settlers waited for stagecoaches; freight piled up under mounds of protective sailcloth awaiting wagon trains.

Within a few weeks a hundred buildings were erected – hotels, warehouses, saloons, and bordellos. North Platte became the first of the wild, riproaring railroad towns that would follow the tracks to the West. Gamblers, harlots, and other camp followers who had preyed upon soldiers during the Civil War at last found them again in North Platte.

'The larger part of the floating population is made up of desperadoes,' reported one correspondent, 'who spend their time in gambling of all kinds, from cards to keno to faro. Day and night the saloons are in full blast, and sums of money varying from five dollars to fifty and even one hundred change hands with a rapidity astonishing to one who is not accustomed to the reck-lessness which their wild frontier life invariably begets.' A traveller passing through North Platte that winter noted laconi-cally: 'Law is unknown here.' And then he added that the in-habitants 'were having a good time gambling, drinking, and shooting each other.'

When Henry Morton Stanley, then a reporter for the *Missouri Democrat*, stepped off the train at North Platte the following spring he found the place in a lively uproar. 'Every gambler in the Union seems to have steered his course for North Platte, and every known game under the sun is played here. The days of Pike's Peak and California are revived. Every house is a saloon, and every saloon is a gambling den. Revolvers are in great re-quisition. Beardless youths imitate to the life the peculiar swagger of the devil-may-care bull-whacker and blackleg ... On account of the immense frighting done to Idaho, Montana, Utah, Dakota, and Colorado, hundreds of bull-whackers walk about, and turn the one street into a perfect Babel. Old gamblers who revelled in the glorious days of "flush times" in the gold districts, declare that this town outstrips all yet.'

Although the track layers went into winter quarters in Novem-ber, they continued to lay rails when weather permitted, and at year's end Jack Casement reported that the track reached to Milepost 305. For the new year of 1867, the Union Pacific also acquired a new president, old John A. Dix having departed to serve as minister to France. For Dix's replacement, Durant the kingmaker chose the wealthy Massachusetts shovelmaker, Oliver Ames, brother of Congressman Oakes Ames. At the UP meeting that elected Oliver Ames president, Oakes Ames sponsored a new director. He was fifty-five-year-old Sidney Dillon, who had been a railroader all his working life, and who had scented the money in Durant's Credit Mobilier. Soon after he became a director in the company, Dillon and the Ames brothers began buying up as many shares of Credit Mobilier as they could find loose on the underground market. Soon they would challenge the financial dictatorship of Dr Durant.

Meanwhile in California, without benefit of very much publicity in the East, the Central Pacific seemed to be playing the role of tortoise in the race with the suddenly harelike Union Pacific. On the day that the UP laid its first rail at Omaha (10 July 1865) the CP was fifty miles out of Sacramento and was building an advance camp at Cisco, forty-two miles farther up the western slope of the Sierras. Sacramento lay at thirty feet above sea level, Cisco at almost six thousand, which explains the difficulties the graders, bridge builders, and tunnellers faced in bringing an Iron Horse to the seven-thousand-foot elevation of the Sierra summit before it could descend to the Nevada plateau. (The owners of the CP were somewhat compensated for this difficult passage by receiving $48,000 per mile from the government as compared with the $16,000 per mile the UP received for its track across the level plains.)

Another major problem faced by the Central Pacific was a shortage of labour. Most Californians could earn more than the two or three dollars per day that the railroad offered, and arrivals from the East tended to seek their fortunes in gold and silver mines. The CPs oxlike general superintendent, Charlie Crocker, stormed about in a futile search for labourers until he finally decided to employ some Chinese out of San Francisco. He took the idea to his construction superintendent, James Harvey Strobridge, who indignantly refused. Strobridge was a professional railroad builder, a Vermont Irishman with the same compulsion to get things done as Jack and Dan Casement, and he did not hold a high regard for Crocker, the former dry-goods merchant. Strobridge had started as a track layer on the Fitchburg Railroad, which ran near Walden Pond, but by the time the whistles of the Iron Horses on that line were annoying Henry Thoreau, he was on his way to California to dig for gold. Instead of becoming a miner, he worked on short-line railways, and Crocker hired him in 1864. The two men had much in common, being bluff, direct, physically powerful, and inclined to settle arguments with their fists.

At first Strobridge scorned Crocker's proposal to hire Chinese to build a railroad. Crocker, however, pointed out that they would work for thirty-five dollars a month, much cheaper than the drifters they were using and who were always threatening to strike. But the Chinese were too frail, Strobridge protested, they ate nothing but rice; no Chinaman was strong enough to move earth and stone and dig tunnels. 'Did they not build the Chinese Wall,' Crocker shouted, 'the biggest piece of masonry in the world?' Strobridge had to admit they had. 'All right,' he said, 'let's hire fifty Chinese on a trial basis. If they can't cut the mustard, that's it.'

After Strobridge had worked the first gang of Chinese for a long twelve-hour day, he notified Crocker to send him fifty more. Within a few weeks Crocker had agents out in all the California towns, signing up every Chinese male they could find. Strobridge, who would have readily admitted to being a slave driver, said that they were the best workers in the world. 'They learn quickly, do not fight, have no strikes that amount to anything, and are very cleanly in their habits. They will gamble, and do quarrel among themselves most noisily – but harmlessly.' At the end of 1865, after the Central Pacific had employed virtually every able-bodied Chinese in California, the railroad's president, Leland Stanford, was attempting to import fifteen thousand more from China.

Popular though the Chinese may have been with the owners of the CP, they were heartily disliked by the other workers, many of whom would throw down their tools and walk away at sight of the Chinese dressed in their neat blue-dyed cotton clothing and umbrella-shaped basket hats. When Samuel Bowles of the *Springfield* (Mass) *Republican* visited the Central Pacific in the summer of 1865, he was told that of the four thousand men at work on the railroad, nine-tenths were Chinese, and that five thousand more Chinese would soon be employed.

Bowles was one of several newspapermen travelling with Schuyler Colfax, then Speaker of the House of Representatives and soon to become Vice-President under President Ulysses Grant. Like all congressmen, Colfax enjoyed travelling luxuriously at government expense, and on this particular junket he was probably making up his mind which end of the transcontinental railroad would offer the most returns for his political insight and favours. The Central Pacific had its own version of the Union Pacific's money-making Credit Mobilier; it was called the Credit and Finance Corporation, but it was even more closely held than Credit Mobilier. The Big Four – Stanford, Huntington, Crocker, and Hopkins – kept this golden goose all to themselves. They acknowledged the visit of the Speaker of the House of Representatives by giving the name Colfax to a station at the end of track, to perpetuate his memory as a friend of railroad owners. But this was not enough for the Speaker. He preferred cash above honours, and back in Washington he eagerly accepted a bundle of Credit Mobilier stock from his fellow congressman Oakes Ames, and thus became a loyal friend of the Union Pacific.

Because of distance and relative inaccessibility, the Central Pacific was unable to compete with the Union Pacific in free excursions for politicians, financiers, and newspapermen, but it did serve as a useful model to inspire Union Pacific employees to work longer and harder. After the Central Pacific won the right from Congress in 1866 to extend its tracks as far beyond the California-Nevada border as was necessary to meet the Union Pacific tracks, Crocker and Strobridge began driving their workmen as hard as the Casement brothers were driving theirs. Each mile covered by iron rails immediately turned into money and land, and the greed of each competing company was intensified by the race across the continent, thus proving that there is nothing like a sense of rivalry to make men commit reckless deeds in war and in love, in business or in engineering.

As the Chinese rolled tons of earth and stone in wheelbarrows to build embankments around the sides of mountains and chipped away at the granite rock of tunnels, the Big Four fretted over the slow pace at which track miles were being added across the Sierras. In the autumn of 1866, while the Union Pacific was leaping a mile a day across the level plains, the Central Pacific work crews climbed doggedly yard by yard towards the snow-clad summits. In November they reached Cisco, ninety-two miles from Sacramento. Determined to use the winter for tunnelling, Strobridge hauled hundreds of Chinese a dozen miles up the wagon road and put them to work digging, blasting, and hauling away the rock debris at both ends of Summit Tunnel, designed to run a quarter of a mile through the stony heart of the last mountain.

To mark the new year of 1867, the *Sacramento Union* reported that the Central Pacific was in daily operation to Cisco, '5,911 feet above the level of the sea – a higher altitude than is attained by any other railroad in America ... Twelve tunnels, varying from 800 to 1,650 feet in length, are in process of construction along the snow belt between the summit and Truckee River, and are being worked night and day by three shifts of men, eight hours each, every twenty-four hours – employing in these tunnels an aggregate of 8,000 labourers.'

In the snows of the Sierras and the blizzards of the Great Plains, the race slowed perceptibly, but the coming of spring 1867 would see its renewal, a continuation of the greatest engineering and construction effort undertaken since the arrival of the first Europeans on the American continent.

FIVE

The Era of the Cowboy is Born

Soon after the Kansas railroad known as the UP Eastern Division lost the race to the 100th meridian, its directors decided to change the name to Kansas Pacific Railroad and to petition Congress for permission to alter the survey of its original route. Instead of turning northwestward into Nebraska to connect with the main line of the Union Pacific, the Kansas Pacific would continue straight west up the valley of the Smoky Hill River and then on to Denver.

By taking the Smoky Hill route, the railroad intruded upon the heartland of Indian hunting country; the food preserve of numerous tribes and subtribes of the Sioux, Cheyenne, and Arapaho. For this reason, from 1867 to 1869 Indian resistance on the Kansas plains reached a peak, and although tradition has it that workers on the Union Pacific were under constant attack from Indians, the men who bore the brunt of these skirmishes were workers on the *Eastern Division*, or the Kansas Pacific. (Not until 1880 was this railroad finally merged permanently with the Union Pacific.)

'From Leavenworth I took railway to Topeka, fifty-eight miles,' wrote Albert D. Richardson in the autumn of 1866. 'The road climbs ridges like saw-teeth; jolts one like corduroys, and rocks him like a rough cradle. It leads through the old Delaware reservation, not long open to settlement, but great cornfields and herds of cattle already appear. The remaining members of this and other Kansas tribes will soon be removed to the Indian Territory, or some other remote region. The whites want their lands – and have the power.'

Later that year, the railroad's tracks reached Fort Riley, where Lieutenant-Colonel George Armstrong Custer had just arrived to assist in the organization of the Seventh Cavalry; the regiment's reason for being was to drive the Plains Indians from the path of the railway. In that same autumn, William J. Palmer organized an excursion party to rival that of Durant and Train in Nebraska. As treasurer and director of construction of the road, Palmer became its driving force after John C. Frémont left it to sink the remainder of his fortune in the Atlantic & Pacific Railroad.

One of those many youthful brigadier generals produced by the recent Civil War, William Palmer's chief claim to fame was that he had led a Pennsylvania cavalry unit in pursuit of the fleeing President of the Confederacy, Jefferson Davis, and had assisted in his capture. Palmer was still in his twenties, dynamic, handsome, and unusually belligerent for a man of Quaker antecedents. A decade later he would be involved in the first Western railroad war, an armed conflict between the Santa Fe and the Denver & Rio Grande.

In 1866, Palmer's job was to raise money for completion of the railroad into Denver. To impress prospective financial backers and the accompanying newspaper writers, Palmer arranged for them to travel in one of George Pullman's first experimental 'sleeping cars', which they boarded in Chicago. 'The car cost twenty thousand dollars!' one of the passengers exclaimed, and he was even more astonished to learn that Pullman was spending thirty thousand on a more advanced model. 'Every comfort which can be placed in such a vehicle is to be found within its wooden walls. The seats, the sides of the car and the ceiling are exquisitely adorned in *marquetrie* or inlaid woods, while the gilded glass frames, in *ormolu*, and the general tone of colour, are truly artistic. It is heated by a separate furnace beneath, and its lounges and mirrors, with every other luxury, make it in fact a rolling palace.'

For most of the journey across Kansas to Fort Riley, the party was awash in champagne, the constant popping of corks accompanied by 'the merry laughter of lady voices'. As there was no dining car or station restaurants west of Topeka, the train stopped occasionally for the cooks to build a fire beside the track and prepare open-air meals of buffalo steaks and other choice viands. At Fort Riley they found the end of track, but they journeyed on by stagecoach to inspect part of the fifty miles of grading that ran straight towards the Colorado line.

One of the reporters was so delighted by the energetic enterprise, and by the vitality and buoyancy of spirits that he found everywhere along the railroad, that he resolved to abandon his plans to travel in Europe and instead return later to follow the track farther westward. 'The world,' he said philosophically, 'in each of its great stages of development has had one *grand route*, which has been the real world of man while it lasted.' After listing several famed travellers' routes used in past centuries, he added: 'Now we are building another road – the most wonderful of all – through regions once unknown, and men call it the Pacific Railway.'

That General Palmer's excursion was helpful in raising more cash was indicated by a burst of energetic building that resumed along the line early in 1867. By March the rails were laid into Abilene, and in June they reached the north bank of Smoky Hill River, eighty-three miles west of Fort Riley. Here was another military post, Fort Ellsworth. For some reason the name was changed to Fort Harker and a land speculator divided the ground to the west into town lots and named the village Ellsworth. When Henry M. Stanley reported its birth for his St Louis newspaper, he wrote: 'The population of the town of Ellsworth is estimated at forty men, four women, eight boys and seven girls. There are also fourteen horses, and about twenty-nine and one-half dogs ... As Ellsworth is part and parcel of this great and progressive country, it is also progressive – for no sooner has the fifth house begun to erect its stately front above the green earth, than the population is gathered in the three saloons to gravely discuss the propriety of making the new town a city, and of electing a mayor.' Neither Stanley nor anyone else could have foreseen that within six years, thousands of Longhorn cattle and hundreds of cowboys coming up the trails from Texas would change Ellsworth into a wild and woolly cow town.

'Wonderful indeed, is the rapidity with which the rolling hills are cleft, roads graded, ties laid down, and the rails secured to their places by the railroad-makers,' Stanley continued. 'Squads of Irishmen under energetic taskmasters, are scattered all along working with might and main as if they had an interest in the road apart from their daily bread or monthly wages. "Excelsior" is the motto all round, and westward do empire and civilization wend their way.'

The 'squads of Irishmen' in the advance construction camps increased to twelve hundred men, and General Palmer ran low on bacon and beef with which to feed them. His meat contractors, Goddard Brothers of Kansas City, sent out a twenty-one-year-old marksman named William F. Cody to hunt buffalo for the workmen. For five hundred dollars a month young Cody guaranteed to supply all the buffalo meat the construction gangs could consume. One day a hunting party of Army officers from Fort Harker came upon a herd of eleven buffalo, but before they could bring their rifles into action, they saw Cody come up at a gallop and slay the entire herd with twelve shots. According to legend, the amazed officers nicknamed the Kansas Pacific's meat hunter Buffalo Bill, and so was born one of the American West's most enduring folk heroes.

Contemporary with Buffalo Bill the hunter and scout was the American cowboy. Undoubtedly the cowboy would have flourished at some time in the late nineteenth century, but the Kansas Pacific Railroad brought him upon the scene early with the establishment of cattle shipping points in towns west of the settled areas – Abilene, Ellsworth, and finally Hays City. The first of the Kansas Pacific's cattle towns was Abilene. When Joseph McCoy, an Illinois livestock trader, arrived there in the early summer of 1867 he described it as 'a very small, dead place consisting of about one dozen log huts, low, small rude affairs, four-fifths of which were covered with dirt for roofing ... The business of the burg was conducted in two small rooms, mere log huts, and of course the inevitable saloon, also in a log hut, could be found.'

McCoy's visit to Abilene had been brought about by a livestock debacle in 1866, the first year in which Texans drove large herds of Longhorn cattle north in search of markets after the Civil War. The markets were there; in fact, a shortage of beef existed in the postwar North. Transportation was the problem; there were no railroads south of Missouri and Kansas. Although the Texans overcame the difficulties of driving their cattle overland through storms and across the rivers of Indian territory, as soon as they reached the settled areas of eastern Kansas they encountered real trouble. Between them and the nearest railheads the country was being homesteaded by farmers, many of them recent battlefield enemies of the Texans. The settlers did not want their fences wrecked and their crops trampled, and they used force in stopping the Texans from driving cattle across their properties. By summer's end of 1866, hundreds of thousands of cattle were stalled between Indian territory and the nearest Missouri railhead. The grass was quickly grazed off, and herds died or were abandoned before they could be sold.

To Joseph McCoy, who was eager to buy cattle for the expanding Chicago meat-packing industry, and to the Texans who wanted to sell cattle, the westward thrust of the Kansas Pacific Railroad offered a solution to the dilemma. McCoy chose Abilene because it was beyond settled farming country, because it bordered a river full of water for thirsty cattle, and because a sweeping sea of grass for miles around could be used for holding and fattening stock at the end of overland drives. To reach Abilene, the Texas cattlemen had only to follow a trail from Red River to the Wichita trading posts on the Arkansas, a trail pioneered by a Cherokee trader named Jesse Chisholm. Chisholm's Trail it was called, and it ran north from the Chickasaw Nation across the relatively shallow Washita, Canadian, and Cimarron rivers.

From the Wichita trading posts, Abilene and the Kansas Pacific Railroad lay a hundred miles farther north across a treeless plain, and while McCoy was building a shipping yard and a three-storey hotel from lumber brought all the way from Hannibal, Missouri, a surveyor was extending the Chisholm Trail. Using a compass and a flagman, the surveyor ran a straight line of heaped-up earthen mounds that the Texas trail drivers could follow from the Arkansas River to Abilene. Late in the summer the first herds came in, and on 5 September the first shipment of twenty cattle cars rumbled eastward on the railroad. Before the brief season ended, thirty-five thousand cattle were driven into Abilene. During the following winter, McCoy sent agents across Texas to distribute circulars and place advertisements in newspapers extolling the advantages of Abilene as a cattle-shipping point. The season of 1868 began early, with endless lines of Longhorns splashing across the Smoky Hill River into Abilene's loading pens. Each year the numbers doubled, the Kansas Pacific being hard-pressed to find enough cars in which to ship out the cattle.

Abilene boomed into a town of forty saloons. Legions of audacious Texans rode up the Chisholm Trail to that garish trail oasis, where they celebrated the end of their overland journeys with whisky, dance-hall girls, and gambling. At first the riders were called 'drovers' or simply 'Texans' (McCoy named his hotel the Drover's Cottage) but soon they were 'cowboys' and they made songs about themselves – 'I'm Bound to Follow the Longhorn Cows', 'The Dying Cowboy', 'Get Along Little Dogies', 'The Old Chisholm Trail', and of course 'The Railroad Corral', in which they sang about rousting steers from the long chaparral and driving them far to the railroad corral, using the tune of 'The Irish Washerwoman'.

Joe McCoy was proud of what he had accomplished. To him it was a successful business venture, nothing more. He probably never realized that he and the KP Railroad on its way to the Western Sea had played a large part in the creation of that most romantic folk creature of the New World – the American cowboy. Without the railroad and the trail town, the image of the cowboy never would have become fully formed. He would have been only a stock handler on horseback, a man wearing a big hat, a bandanna, boots and spurs. Without the trail town he would have had no destination, no relationship with the Calico Queens and Painted Cats, the dance-hall girls of a dozen Bull's Head Taverns & Gambling Saloons, Long Branches, Alamos, and Lady Gays. He would have had no town marshals to challenge to the death in thousands of legendary walkdowns and shoot-outs on the Texas Streets that fronted the railroad tracks. He might have lived and died without ever seeing the steaming, smoking Iron Horse that hauled away the bawling Longhorns he drove up from Texas. Without the Iron Horse, the trail town, and the cowboy, a larger part of the myth of the American West would have faded into history, never to be perpetuated in multitudes of yellow-backed dime novels and millions of feet of film flicking shadows on motion-picture and television screens.

The American Indian was there, too, cast in the villain's role of Cowboys & Indians, the stereotyped conflict immortalized in a children's game that has become a universal symbol of good and evil. Along the Chisholm Trail and other overland routes to the railroad towns, cowboys and Indians occasionally exchanged gunfire. More often than not, the Indians wanted nothing more than a few beeves to replace the buffalo that the cattlemen had driven from their land; sometimes the tribes of Indian territory demanded a toll (ten cents per head was the going rate) for Longhorns crossing their reservations. Cowboys and Indians seldom sought out each other; the shifting overland cattle trails usually ran west of settlement but east of the Plains tribes' hunting grounds. As the tribes were pushed west, the trails moved west behind them.

A few hundred railroad workers in Kansas and Nebraska probably took more punishment from Indians than did all the thousands of cowboys from Texas to Montana. It was the Iron Horse that the warriors hated, the snorting, whistling monster that violated their natural sanctuary and drove away their wild game. As soon as iron tracks invaded the High Plains west of Salina, the Indians began to fight, challenging surveyors, graders, track layers, and even train crews. In the spring and summer of 1867, hunting parties of Cheyenne, Sioux, and Arapaho raided along the stretch of track between Ellsworth and Fort Hays. Graders at Wilson's Creek and Bunker Hill took casualties in several attacks during June, and farther west at Monument Station a thousand men exchanged their shovels for rifles and refused to work until a regiment of Kansas volunteer cavalrymen arrived to shield them from angry swarms of Plains Indians. At Brookville, only sixteen miles west of Salina, a war party surrounded a temporary roundhouse containing a locomotive and train crew, and then tried to set the building afire. In an attempt to escape, the engineer got up steam and crashed his Iron Horse through the flimsy roundhouse door. The noise of splintering wood and the appearance of the hated monster with its shrilling whistle and jangling bell frightened the attackers into hasty flight.

Reacting to this determined resistance to the railroad by the Plains Indians, General William T. Sherman ordered an expedition into the area, under the direction of General Winfield Scott Hancock. Sherman, who was in command of military forces in the West, had devised a plan to drive all the Plains Indians north of the Platte and south of the Arkansas River, leaving a broad belt between for the transcontinental railroads and ultimate settlement of the Indian lands that the roads would acquire as they laid their tracks westward. During the summer of 1867, Hancock with George Armstrong Custer of the Seventh Cavalry chased Indians across Kansas, burning tepee villages and killing indiscriminately. By autumn the Great Plains on both sides of the Kansas Pacific Railroad was in a turmoil that signalled the beginning of a long and bloody Indian war.

Although Hancock was recalled and the federal government through its Interior Department attempted to pacify the aroused tribes with treaty signings at Medicine Lodge, Kansas, and Fort Laramie, Wyoming, the more militant Indian leaders remained adamant against the railroads. Small war parties continued raiding, the most effective group consisting of about two hundred Cheyenne Dog Soldiers with a few Sioux and Arapaho allies. A visitor to the town of Sheridan at the end of track in 1868 reported that the place was in a state of siege. 'Several days before, a large war party of savages had appeared upon two buttes near the town and opened fire upon the inhabitants. Everybody rushed to arms, and for the larger part of the day a spirited fusillade was kept up. The people of the place at once recognized a regular corps of defenders, and detachments were on the watch day and night. On the more prominent eminences pickets were posted to signal the approach of war parties. At night the guard was doubled so as to completely encircle the town.'

In a move to punish the resisting Indians, Sherman now sent the famous Civil War cavalry commander Philip Sheridan out upon the plains. Believing that the only good Indian was a dead Indian, Sheridan recruited a special company of frontier scouts at Fort Hays and ordered them to track down and kill any Indians sighted near the railroad. In September the scouts trailed a large band of Cheyenne Dog Soldiers to the Arikara fork of the Republican River. There the Indians trapped the scouts on an island and kept them surrounded for eight days until a relief column arrived. During the fighting, the famous warrior Roman Nose and Lieutenant Frederick Beecher were killed. History recorded the incident as the Battle of Beecher's Island, but the Indians called it the Fight When Roman Nose Was Killed. Continuing his war to crush Indian resistance completely, Sheridan organized a winter campaign under Lieutenant-Colonel Custer, which culminated on 27 November in the destruction of Black Kettle's peaceful Cheyenne village. Although there was practically no resistance, the Army glorified the incident by calling it the Battle of the Washita.

The ranks of the railroad defiers were growing thin now among the High Plains tribes. Through the spring of 1869, Tall Bull and his unyielding Dog Soldiers and a few small bands of Sioux and Arapaho managed to elude their pursuers. For a few weeks they fought a desperate last-ditch guerrilla war against the Iron Horse.

On 28 May, about thirty Cheyennes armed with rifles and bows caught seven track repairmen west of Fossil Creek Station (now Russell, Kansas). One of the workmen, Adolph Roenigk, said the Indians came dashing out of a ravine 'yelling like demons'. Roenigk and his companions grabbed their rifles and ran for a handcar. 'We tried to get the car under headway, but had gone only a short distance when more Indians came out of the ravine ahead of us, and the next minute we were surrounded and they were firing into us from all sides ... I thought it impossible to reach the station alive. The Indians were pressing us hard. When their guns were empty and no time to reload, we received a shower of arrows.' (Artist Jacob Gogolin later painted scenes of this incident from Roenigk's descriptions.) Before the railroad workmen were halfway to the safety of the station dugout, two of them were shot and fell from the handcar. Four of the five survivors were wounded, and only the intercession of the station agent with his Spencer carbine enabled them to reach the dugout.

Some of the Indians kept the repairmen pinned down there while others tore up a section of track by breaking off the heads of spikes and removing several rails. After darkness fell, the besieged railroad men could still hear sounds of the Indians and their ponies. Near midnight, the headlight of an approaching train appeared on the eastern horizon. To warn the engineer of the broken rails, the station agent tossed a bale of hay onto the middle of the track and set it afire. The engineer, however, did not sight the blaze in time to avoid overturning into a ditch. Thus did the Cheyennes hamper the Iron Horse. But they could not destroy that hated symbol of the white man's technology; two days later, a wrecking crew lifted the monster back up on its repaired tracks and brought it once again to steaming life.

A hundred miles farther west and about two weeks later, a similar party (possibly the same warriors) ripped up the track near Grinnell. When the locomotive of the eastbound train was derailed, the Indians swarmed down upon the cars, but by this time the Kansas Pacific had introduced the practice of arming its passengers. A volley of shots from the car windows forced the attackers into a hasty retreat.

Surveyors, being the 'point men' of an advancing railroad, were viewed as hostile spies by the people whose country they were marking off for invasion. Because of constant attacks upon them as the Kansas Pacific moved west from Fort Wallace into Colorado, surveyors refused to go into the field without the protection of at least a platoon of soldiers. And if the engineers grew careless in their work, this armed guard offered little security.

'We were running some rapid trial lines north of Sheridan, and were fifteen or twenty miles out in a rolling country,' a transit man recorded in June 1869. 'Our progress was as rapid almost as a man would walk at a moderate pace, and we were exceedingly vulnerable to attack, as we were all separated, strung out over a distance of a mile or more.' The man in front that day was Philip Schuyler, a twenty-five-year-old engineer. He was on horseback, riding slowly to choose the best grade route, when he suddenly discovered that he was entering a V-shaped ambush with mounted Indians swarming up from left and right out of deep narrow ravines. A bullet flesh-wounded Schuyler's horse, and what followed was one of those classic chases so relished by writers of Western fiction and directors of Western cinema.

Putting spurs to his horse, Schuyler forced the animal to leap across one awesome ravine after another, but just as he thought he was escaping to level ground, another formidable array of Indians blocked his passage and he was again quickly surrounded. The circling warriors rode closer and closer, shaking their weapons and taunting the young engineer. Schuyler raised his rifle and fired at the nearest man. As the Indian fell, Schuyler spurred his horse into a sudden charge and broke through the line. In the pursuit that followed, Schuyler's bleeding horse was wounded again, his field glass was shot away, bullets struck the breech of his rifle and pierced his clothing, and the shaft of a hurled lance almost knocked him from his saddle. To add a cinematic finish to the incident, when Schuyler at last reached his fellow surveyors, he found them engaged in a fight with another war party and had to help drive away these attackers. 'We were unanimous in the opinion that it was folly to continue work without a larger escort and a personal bodyguard,' the transit man recorded. 'Consequently it was decided to turn our faces in the direction of Sheridan, which we did, arriving there late in the afternoon, the Indians following us all the way.'

During the month succeeding this incident, several cavalry columns patrolled the railroad and combed the High Plains with orders 'to treat all Indians as hostile'. On 11 July 1869, eight troops of cavalry and a battalion of Pawnee mercenaries stormed Tall Bull's summer encampment at Summit Springs. They charged in a double encirclement from east and west, trapping the Cheyennes in a deadly crossfire, and when the assault ended a few minutes later, Tall Bull and most of his defiant young haters of the railroad were dead. From that day, the Iron Horse thundered freely across the High Plains of Kansas.

During the Hancock and Custer campaign along the Kansas Pacific in 1867, a number of Indian raiders shifted their operations northward to the Union Pacific in Nebraska. There they achieved only one notable success, the legendary train ambush at Plum Creek on 6 August. Long afterwards, a Cheyenne named Porcupine told why they wrecked the train: 'The soldiers had defeated us and taken everything that we had and had made us poor. We were feeling angry and said among ourselves that we ought to do something. In these big wagons that go on this metal road, there must be things that are valuable – perhaps clothing. If we could throw these wagons off the iron they run on and break them open, we should find out what was in them and could take whatever might be useful to us.'

The day after the wreck occurred, Henry M. Stanley happened to be in Omaha, and he interviewed a survivor, a fellow Briton named William Thompson, who worked for the Union Pacific as a telegraph repairman. Thompson and four other men had been sent out after nightfall on a handcar from Plum Creek to find and repair a break in the telegraph line. Unknown to them, the wire had been torn down by Porcupine and the other Cheyennes, and part of it was used to fasten a railroad tie to the track. The tie was meant to derail an Iron Horse, but instead the handcar carrying the telegraph repairmen struck it and the Indians rose up out of the high grass to surround the men.

In the pursuit that followed, four of the five repairmen were quickly killed. A Cheyenne shot Thompson in the arm, knocked him to the ground, and then scalped him. Although the pain was excruciating, Thompson pretended to be unconscious. 'I can't describe it to you,' he told Stanley. 'It just felt as if the whole head was taken right off. The Indian then mounted and galloped away, but as he went he dropped my scalp within a few feet of me, which I managed to get and hide. The Indians were thick in the vicinity, or I might then have made my escape. While lying down I could hear the Indians moving around whispering to each other, and then shortly after placing obstructions on the track. After lying down about an hour and a half I heard the low rumbling of the train as it came tearing along, and I might have been able to flag it off had I dared.'

The Iron Horse and several freight cars plunged into the ditch, killing the engineer and fireman. The conductor and three other men in the caboose escaped and ran back down the track to warn a second freight train, which was following close behind the first. William Thompson meanwhile took advantage of the Cheyennes' preoccupation with the loot that they were digging out of the wrecked freight cars. He crawled away through the grass, still clutching his scalp, and then jogged fifteen miles to Willow Island Station. After his fellow workers dressed his wounds, Thompson made his way to Omaha, carrying his scalp in a pail of water to prevent it from drying out. 'The scalp,' reported the observant Stanley, 'was about nine inches in length and four in width, somewhat resembling a drowned rat as it floated, curled up, on the water.' Thompson hoped to find a doctor who could reset it on his head, but the effort failed. He then had his scalp tanned, and after returning to England, for some reason known only to himself, he shipped it back to Omaha, where it was exhibited for years in the public library's museum.

Reprisals upon the Union Pacific such as the Cheyennes' Plum Creek ambush were abominations to General Sherman, who had come to regard the railroad as a holy endeavour that must be defended at all costs against such 'a worthless set of scamps' as the Plains Indians. He ordered out more infantry units to guard the graders and track layers and more cavalrymen to patrol the completed tracks. 'No interruption to work upon the line of the UP will be tolerated,' he assured Dr Durant. 'Eastern people must not allow their sympathy with the Indians to make them forget what is due to those who are pushing the "frontier" further and further west. These men deserve protection and they must have it.'

One of the railroad's medical officers reported from Fort Sedgwick that military protection seemed adequate but that 'the Indians laugh and hoot at the infantry and boldly ride within reach of their muskets, then ducking under the bellies of their fleet ponies pat their breech clouts defiantly. They seem to exhibit more respect for the cavalry.'

As an example of the railroad company's hardening attitude towards Indian resistance to invasion of their hunting areas, the scalps of Sioux and Cheyenne Indians taken by the hired Pawnee scouts were displayed freely to travellers. George Francis Train obtained a scalp that still had an ear attached, and during an 1867 springtime excursion he enjoyed startling the Easterners by exhibiting it along with the arrow that had killed its luckless owner.

The excursionists on this tour were the first to journey by rail all the way to Council Bluffs; the Chicago & Northwestern had at last brought its tracks to the Missouri River, which the travellers easily crossed by ferry to the muddy streets of Omaha. Those who had come from New York City reached Omaha in only sixty-nine hours, a feat that the newspaper correspondents hailed as epochal. The party was invited to inspect the Union Pacific's recently completed machine shops, which extended three miles along the bank of the Missouri and contained stalls for twenty locomotives, and their car works, which turned out two flatcars and one freight car each day and was beginning construction of crude passenger cars for the use of immigrants who would soon be arriving to buy hundreds of thousands of acres of the railroad's land along the right-of-way.

Two hundred ninety miles to the west, or twelve hours by train, North Platte was sobering up from its winter of gambling, drinking, and fornicating, and was preparing to move westward. The energetic Casement brothers established a new camp near Julesburg, Colorado, and put two thousand graders to work; they hired eighteen hundred woodchoppers and haulers and sent them to the forested areas of Wyoming. By the season's end they would have 100,000 ties ready for the rails entering Wyoming. As midsummer approached, North Platte's population shrank from five thousand to three hundred. The gamblers and whores moved on to Julesburg to live off the railroad workmen.

When Henry Stanley visited 'sinful Julesburg' in August 1867, he found a comfortable hotel filled with well-dressed guests. 'Everybody had gold watches attached to expensive chains, and several wore patent leather boots. I vow I thought they were great capitalists, but was astonished to find they were only clerks, ticket agents, conductors, engineers ... I walked on till I came to a dance-house, bearing the euphonious title of "King of the Hills", gorgeously decorated and brilliantly lighted ... The ground floor was as crowded as it could well be, and all were talking loud and fast, and mostly everyone seemed bent on debauchery and dissipation. The women appeared to be the most reckless, and the men seemed nothing loth to enter a whirlpool of sin ... The managers of the saloons rake in greenbacks by hundreds every night; there appears to be plenty of money here, and plenty of fools to squander it ... These women are expensive articles, and come in for a large share of the money wasted. In broad daylight they may be seen gliding through the sandy streets in Black Crook dresses, carrying fancy derringers slung to their waists, with which tools they are dangerously expert ... The population of Julesburg is rapidly growing, and the town, like its predecessor of North Platte, may be epitomized as a jumble of commencements, always shifting, never ending.'

Meanwhile, another 140 miles to the west, a new camp was being established on Crow Creek in Wyoming. In honour of the Indian tribe that had challenged the invasion of the Iron Horse with more fury than had any other, the surveyors named the camp Cheyenne. General Grenville Dodge predicted that rails would be laid to Cheyenne before the first snows of winter, but few of his engineers believed this to be possible.

On through the late summer and autumn, the well-organized gangs of workers pushed the rails ever westward, a mile a day, two miles a day, sometimes four miles a day. The rail terminus at Council Bluffs eliminated the slow shipments of iron and other supplies by steamboat up the Missouri. The ferry to Omaha shuttled back and forth with car-loads of rails and spikes that could be loaded right onto the UP tracks for swift passage towards Wyoming. When Dr Henry C. Parry passed through Cheyenne on 7 October, he was astounded at the changes he found there: 'When I left here last July all the land was bare, and the only habitations were tents. Cheyenne has now a population of fifteen hundred, two papers, stores, warehouses, hotels, restaurants, gambling halls, etc.'

All this occurred even before the rails reached Cheyenne. Four thousand people were there a few weeks later when Jack Casement's headquarters train rolled to a stop beside the brand-new Cheyenne station. Awaiting him was a speaker's stand with brilliant banners mounted above it: OLD CASEMENT, WE WELCOME YOU. THE MAGIC CITY GREETS THE CONTINENTAL RAILWAY.

The next day, the first passenger train arrived, and from it poured a considerable portion of the gamblers and dance-hall girls of Julesburg. A few hours later, a long train of flatcars rumbled into the station. Every car was loaded high with knocked-down buildings, storefronts, dance-hall floors, tents, wooden sidings, and entire roofs. According to legend, as a brakeman dropped down onto the station platform, he shouted to the waiting crowd: 'Gentlemen, here's Julesburg!'

It was Samuel Bowles, that widely travelled publisher of the *Springfield* (Mass) *Republican*, who first put into print the name of these movable towns: 'As the Railroad marched thus rapidly across the broad Continent of plain and mountain, there was improvised a rough and temporary town at its every public stopping place ... these settlements were of the most perishable materials, – canvas tents, plain board shanties, and turf-hovels, – pulled down and sent forward for a new career, or deserted as worthless, at every grand movement of the Railroad company ... Restaurant and saloon keepers, gamblers, desperadoes of every grade, the vilest of men and women made up this "Hell on Wheels", as it was most aptly termed.' Thus did the Hell on Wheels town enter the American language.

At the end of 1867, the Union Pacific was 540 miles from Omaha, 240 miles closer to the Western Sea than it had been in January. Almost every citizen of the nation gloried in this mighty achievement, but there were exceptions. Dr Thomas Durant was unhappy because Oliver Ames and Sidney Dillon voted him off the board of directors of Credit Mobilier and were boldly attempting to remove him as executive vice-president and general manager of the UP. And so began a power struggle for access to the fountains of gold flowing from the building of the 'people's' transcontinental railroad.

The men most disturbed by the remarkable progress of the Union Pacific were the Big Four of the Central Pacific. In 1867, while the UP was laying two hundred forty miles of track, the CP laid only forty miles. To accomplish this, Crocker's and Strobridge's Chinese workers had to bore thousands of feet through the solid stone of the Sierras and move thousands of cubic yards of gravel in wheelbarrows, while fighting snowdrifts and dodging avalanches during several months of the year. This was substantially the same barrier that had tragically stopped the Donner party coming from the East twenty years earlier; those California-bound emigrants were reduced to cannibalism before rescuers reached them.

Learning that an engineer spying for the Union Pacific had visited the tunnel sites and reported that three years would be required to complete Summit Tunnel alone, the resourceful Strobridge ordered a shaft sunk so that his tunnellers could dig from four sides simultaneously. For several months during 1867 he kept eight thousand Chinese tunnellers working in around-the-clock shifts seven days a week. Nevertheless, there were rumours from

New York that Dr Durant was boasting that the Union Pacific would reach the California line before the Central Pacific could work its way out of the Sierras.

Reacting to this with their usual ingenuity, the Big Four decided to bypass the tunnels temporarily and push the Central Pacific tracks down the eastern slope of the Sierras and across the line into the level Nevada desert. Once there, they could sweep across the miles to Salt Lake City before the Union Pacific track layers reached Utah.

To accomplish this, Strobridge took three thousand Chinese over the summit to grade and bridge the eastern slope to the Nevada line. But the greatest feat of all was the dismantling of three locomotives and forty cars and the transportation of them over the summit on sledges. It was an accomplishment equal to Hannibal's crossing of the ice-clad Alps, with the Iron Horses sliding and foundering in the snow somewhat like Hannibal's armoured elephants.

'We hauled locomotives over,' general manager Crocker later recalled, 'and when I say we, I mean myself. We hauled them on sleighs ... we hauled some of them over on logs, because we could not get a sleigh big enough.' After the Iron Horses and their tenders and cars were brought slipping and sliding down the slope, they had to be loaded onto wagons at Donner Lake and dragged along a rough and muddy road to Truckee. And after this was done, a cavalcade of sleds and wagons followed with tons of spikes, ploughs, tools, food supplies, saw mills, and iron rails – enough to lay fifty miles of track.

Adding to the hardships of a difficult year for the Central Pacific were blizzards and avalanches that dumped thirty-foot drifts on the already completed tracks. 'The snow would fill up just as fast as the men could dig it out,' Crocker said. To keep the road open to the summit tunnels, he employed a Scotsman, bridge-builder Arthur Brown, and ordered him to construct forty miles of snowsheds. In completing this assignment, Brown used sixty-five million feet of timber and nine hundred tons of bolts and spikes, and spent over two million dollars.

In November 1867, at the highest point of the Central Pacific, 7,017 feet above sea level, Summit Tunnel was ready for the track layers. A month later, to celebrate their triumph, the Big Four loaded ten bright yellow passenger cars at Sacramento with seven hundred Very Important People of California and hauled them up the 105-mile track to the top of the Sierras. There the excursionists engaged in a snowball fight, and were almost smothered by smoke when the Iron Horse stalled in the long tunnel, but returned safely to Sacramento to spread the news of California's marvellous railroad.

On 13 December, Strobridge and his Chinese workers on the eastern slope of the range laid the first rails across the Nevada line. But the Central Pacific still had to lay a seven-mile stretch of track to close in the Donner Lake area, and it was already buried for the winter under its first snowfall. No subsidy bonds could be collected from the government for the miles completed beyond the gap, because according to the law the tracks had to be *consecutive*. No doubt about it, the Central Pacific was in a financial bind. Back to the East, however, travelled that cold and crafty manoeuverer of politicians and financiers – Collis Huntington. He stretched the Big Four's credit to the limits, ordering railroad equipment in such enormous quantities that at one time thirty ships loaded with iron for the Central Pacific were circling the oceans en route to California. Huntington knew that more than a thousand miles of empty land still lay between the ends of track of the CP and the UP, and he intended to grab for the CP every mile of it that muscle and sweat could accomplish.

SIX

The Great Race

The Great Race actually began in the spring of 1867 at North Platte, Nebraska, but it was no contest until the spring of 1868, when the Central Pacific's Chinese workers came down the eastern slope of the Sierras and began laying grades across the arid flatlands of Nevada towards the Great Basin of Utah. This green and fruitful country of the industrious Mormons was a rich prize, and the Big Four were so determined to win it that they dispatched teams of surveyors as far east as Wyoming, where they encountered the red-flag markers and theodolites of the equally eager Union Pacific surveyors.

Early in the spring of 1868, the CP track layers reached a newly created town named for General Jesse L. Reno of Civil War fame. Because of its strategic location adjacent to the Nevada mining country, twenty-five-foot storefront lots were soon selling for twelve hundred dollars. As soon as a station was built at end of track, construction superintendent James Strobridge shifted his crews back into the melting snows of the Sierras to complete the seven-mile gap between Reno and Sacramento. By mid-June the frozen earth and the stones were blasted and levelled, the rails were spiked down, and the gap was closed. The Big Four could now collect a fortune from the government. A newspaper reporter who was a passenger on the first train to cross the Sierras from Sacramento described the Central Pacific as 'one of the most beautiful, smooth and solid roads on the continent'. The Chinese labourers, he added, were 'packing their traps preparatory to passing on over the summit into the great interior basin of the continent'.

Not only the Chinese workers but also President Leland Stanford of the CP went over the mountains that summer. Stanford's mission was to visit Salt Lake City, where he hoped to persuade Brigham Young and other Mormon leaders to build a road grade across Utah through Weber Canyon to the Wyoming line. That Young already had a $2-million contract with the rival Union Pacific to build a grade across Utah did not matter to Stanford and his Big Four partners. During the previous winter Collis Huntington had filed with the Secretary of the Interior a set of maps for a right-of-way across Nevada and Utah, labelling them as an extension of the Central Pacific line. With his usual audacity, Huntington at the same time asked the government for an advance payment of $2.4 million for construction of the line (which he never built) and he badgered officials for months until he had the bonds in hand.

Brigham Young saw no conflict in taking on two contracts, especially after Stanford guaranteed to pay the Mormons double the wages he had been giving his Chinese workers. The money of course ultimately would come from the republic's taxpayers, most of whom were unaware that during the autumn of 1868 separate crews of Mormons were hard at work hauling stone and earth to build two hundred miles of parallel road grades, one of which would never be used. The Great Race was becoming wasteful and expensive. Yet, most Americans rejoiced in the progress of what they believed to be 'their' transcontinental railroad.

Strobridge and his Chinese in the meantime were driving eastward across Nevada. To avoid conflicts with Indians – such as had hampered the Union Pacific and Kansas Pacific on the Great Plains – the Central Pacific offered some of the native Americans employment and then signed a special treaty with the Paiutes and Shoshonis. 'We gave the old chiefs a pass each, good on the passenger cars,' Huntington said, 'and we told our men to let the common Indians ride on the freight cars whenever they saw fit.' Both male and female Indians worked alongside the Chinese 'with nonchalance and ease', and one observer reported that the women usually outdid the men in handling crowbars and sledgehammers.

On one occasion some of the Paiutes who were working with a Chinese construction gang on the grade between Reno and Wadsworth unintentionally caused a halt in operations. Having a natural fondness for tall tales, the Indians one day told the Orientals that their Nevada desert was inhabited by snakes so large that they could swallow a man in one gulp. The result was a hasty departure that night by about five hundred Chinese, who decided to follow the railroad track back to the safety of Sacramento. An infuriated Charlie Crocker had to dispatch several men on horseback to round up the frightened Chinese and persuade them that they were the victims of Paiute humour.

On 22 July, the tracks reached Wadsworth and soon afterwards the first train from Sacramento rolled into the station. From there the survey line swung northeastward to work its way through the passes of the Humboldt Range. This was the desert country that overland emigrants bound for California had learned to dread. For five hundred miles it was a land of white alkali beds burned by the sun, waterless, treeless, bare of vegetation except for patches of grey sagebrush and stunted junipers. To supply timber for construction and to fuel locomotives, logs had to be hauled from the Sierra forests. Special water trains consisting of huge wooden tanks fitted upon flatcars were devised to bring that vital liquid to workmen and to fill the boilers of the advance contingent of Iron Horses.

To avoid building bridges and digging cuts – which consumed time and money – Crocker and Strobridge ran the line in snake-like curves. Each additional mile of track, after all, brought to the Big Four a profit of twice its cost to them. In a few years, millions more dollars would have to be spent to straighten those winding tracks so hastily and carelessly laid during the Great Race.

In September, after the track layers passed Mill City, a San Francisco reporter made the journey to end of track. He found that the names that the Central Pacific had bestowed upon its stations revealed the nature of the Nevada land: Desert, Hot Springs, Mirage, Granite Point. He also witnessed the lackadaisical manner in which government inspectors examined and certified the new track so that the CP could collect its thirty thousand dollars per mile. One inspector, said the reporter, stood on the platform of the rear car and with a small spyglass scrutinized the ties, rails, and grade as the train sped along. While he was doing this, his assistant lay down on the floor in the front of the car, shut his eyes, and composed himself to sleep. The argument being this, that if the passengers could sleep the track must be level, easy, and all right; whereas, if too rough to sleep, something must be wrong with the work.'

The CP was averaging a mile of new track each day now, racing frantically to beat the UP into Utah. Borrowing the methods of the Casement brothers of the UP, superintendent Strobridge put together a work train of a dozen cars equipped with sleeping and dining accommodations and shops for carpenters and telegraph-line builders. The first car was Strobridge's living quarters, and his wife kept it so neat that a newspaperman dubbed her 'the heroine of the Central Pacific' and declared that the domicile on wheels was equal to any home in San Francisco. A contemporary photograph shows Mrs Strobridge standing on a porchlike platform built along the length of the car; beside her is a clothes-line, hanging from which appears to be a pair of long underdrawers. A Vallejo reporter described the platform as 'an awning veranda' and said that a canary bird swinging at the front door gave it a most homelike appearance. Each evening when Strobridge's work train rolled to the end of track built that day, he would have a telegraph wire run from the nearest pole into the telegraph car and would notify Sacramento of the number of miles of track laid.

No matter how hard he and Crocker drove their men, however, it became obvious as 1868 neared its end that the rival Union Pacific was going to win the Great Race into Utah and probably would have tracks laid to the key city of Ogden before the Central Pacific could push through the Promontory Range north of Great Salt Lake. Much to Brigham Young's displeasure, both railroads had abandoned plans to run their main tracks into Salt Lake City. A branch line from Ogden to Salt Lake, similar to the branch line from Cheyenne to Denver, would have to suffice. Young, however, demanded control of the spur, and he later outfitted it with rolling stock that he took from the UP in partial payment for the Mormons' grading contract.

At year's end the Central Pacific's tracks were approaching Carlin, Nevada, 446 miles from Sacramento; the Union Pacific's rails had been laid to Evanston, Wyoming, near the Utah border, 995 miles west of Omaha. Between these track ends were less than

400 miles, a considerable part of which had been graded in parallel lines by the rival Mormon contractors and Strobridge's Chinese workers. An air of excitement developed across America as it became apparent that the long-dreamed-of transcontinental railroad, which had been planned for completion during the nation's centennial celebration of 1876, would be joined in the new year of 1869, seven years ahead of schedule.

Although engineers for each of the rival railroads could have calculated the approximate meeting place of the track layers, their acquisitive employers insisted that the wasteful parallel grading continue across Utah. Finally, the UP construction men recognized the futility of continuing their grading west of Promontory towards Humboldt Wells in Nevada. After discontinuing work on this section, they brought gangs of Irish graders into Utah so that in the spring of 1869 each railroad company was grading a line between Ogden and Promontory. Grenville Dodge of the UP noted that considerable ill feeling developed between the Irish and the Chinese. 'Our Irishmen were in the habit of firing their blasts in the cuts without giving warning to the Chinamen on the Central Pacific working right above them. From this cause several Chinamen were severely hurt. Complaint was made to me by the Central Pacific people, and I endeavoured to have the contractors bring all hostilities to a close, but, for some reason or other they failed to do so. One day the Chinamen, appreciating the situation, put in what is called a "grave" on their work, and when the Irishmen right under them were all at work let go their blast and buried several of our men. This brought about a truce at once. From that time the Irish labourers showed due respect for the Chinamen, and there was no further trouble.'

The Union Pacific's race to Ogden was not won without enormous costs – in money, materials, and lives. As in war, the longer the contest continued, the more ruthless, reckless, and callous the leaders of the contending railroads became towards their common workmen. Although losses of lives by accidents were higher among the CP's Chinese (between five hundred and a thousand), the UP undoubtedly lost the most workmen from exposure and from diseases contracted in the squalid dens of prostitution that followed the tracks westward. More UP workmen were murdered in the Hell on Wheels towns than were killed in accidents, a ratio of about four to one. Almost no medical facilities were provided by either railroad company. Yet, with the assistance of the national press, the railroad owners, like military commanders in wartime, kept up a drumfire of propaganda upon the populace that was designed to inspire their sweating labourers to 'win' at all costs.

In the spring of 1868, the UP emerged from the long Wyoming winter to begin track construction west of Cheyenne. General Jack Casement's work train was lengthened to eighty cars, which now included a bakery car, a bath car, a complete feed store and saddle shop, additional kitchen, dining, and bunk cars, a combined telegraph and payroll car, and a butcher's car. The butcher's car was kept filled with fresh beef from a cattle herd that was driven each day alongside the work train as it made its way westward across Wyoming. From time to time a newspaper that followed the Hell on Wheels towns would set up shop temporarily in one of the cars, publishing whenever enough news could be collected concerning events along the way combined with occasional brief dispatches received in the telegraph car. For protection in case of Indian attacks, the Casements installed about a thousand rifles upon horizontal racks in the ceilings of the cars. Added protection was guaranteed by the railroad's good friend General Sherman, who ordered five thousand infantrymen and cavalrymen deployed at public expense from Cheyenne to the Salt Lake Valley.

During the winter of 1867-8, the Union Pacific had sent a work force of three thousand men into the Medicine Bow Range to cut ties, timbers for bridge construction, and billets to fuel Iron Horses. As the snows departed, teams of muleskinners began distributing the wood alongside the grades and survey lines. 'Muleskinners,' reported a contemporary observer, 'yelling at reluctant animals, split the air with picturesque invective and creased tough mule hides with the business end of blacksnake whips.'

At the same time, grading crews by the thousands were sent as far west as Echo Canyon in Utah. There was much boastful talk about laying track to Salt Lake before the year's end, but the realists thought the railroad would be lucky to reach the Wasatch Mountains before snow stopped construction. Edward Ordway, who was travelling across Wyoming that spring, encountered at Fort Halleck a group of brawling railroad workmen, 'natives of all the civilized nations of earth,' drinking up their winter's pay at the bar in the sutler's store. 'Rock men, pick and shovellers, and all other necessary helpers in railroad grade making, at that time as a class were known as Navvies,' he said. 'All stout, healthy men, and as for their social standing or moral turpitude, all that is necessary to say is that nature had created them for a special purpose that people more delicately organized were unfit for.'

During their drinking bouts, the men engaged in boxing, clog dancing, and jumping contests. They harassed stagecoach drivers, sang Irish ballads, and then to Ordway's amazement a quartet rendered 'in perfect harmony Hayden's [sic] magnificent song "The Heavens Are Telling"'. The men were enjoying themselves so heartily after their long winter in the timber that the gang bosses were unable to start them back to work without the assistance of a detail of cavalry from the fort, who 'by a liberal use of sabres succeeded in rounding up those who were able to walk'.

During April an army of graders moved out through deep patches of snow into the Wyoming Black Hills, and a thousand track layers followed. On 16 April, iron rails topped Sherman Summit, 8,242 feet above sea level, a thousand feet higher than the Central Pacific's Summit Tunnel in the Sierras. Grenville Dodge had surveyed this pass to the Western Sea in 1865 and named it 'in honour of General Sherman the tallest general in the service'. To celebrate the crossing of what the Union Pacific boasted was the highest elevation ever reached by a railroad anywhere in the world, Dr Durant came out from New York and personally placed the final rail. He could not resist sending a bragging telegram to President Leland Stanford of the Central Pacific, and Stanford politely replied: 'We cheerfully yield you the palm of superior elevation; 7,242 feet has been quite sufficient to satisfy our highest ambition.' By this time Durant was feuding bitterly with his associates Sidney Dillon and Oakes Ames, and was so furious with Grenville Dodge, because of the latter's refusal to cooperate in his devious plots to siphon funds, that Durant had determined to remove Dodge as chief engineer at the first opportunity.

While the owners' celebrated at Sherman Summit, bridge builders a few miles down the western slope were nailing together a framework of timbers 650 feet long and 130 feet high across Dale Creek. It was the largest trestlework on the UP, and when winds blew up the canyon the bridge swayed alarmingly. Government inspectors refused to approve it until they extracted a promise from Durant to lash it down with cables and replace it with an iron structure within one year. 'The highest railroad bridge in the world,' boasted the UP, but to the men who first crossed it on an Iron Horse it was like spanning a structure of interlaced toothpicks.

Bypassing the incompleted bridge, Jack Casement pushed his track layers on towards Laramie City. Silas Seymour, the dandy who was still acting as 'consulting engineer', field agent, and spy for Durant, was in evidence again, accompanied occasionally by a mistress and several black servants. He and Durant were plotting something, but neither Casement nor construction superintendent Sam Reed could yet determine what was in the wind. To pick up some easy money, Durant had the townsite of Laramie surveyed into lots, and Seymour spread rumours that the division shops and roundhouse originally planned by Dodge to be located at Cheyenne would be transferred to Laramie. This of course caused a sharp increase in the demand for Laramie City lots. Within a week, four hundred lots were sold at exorbitant prices, and when the tracks came in early in May, about 8,500 of Cheyenne's 10,000 population and a large number of that town's knockdown buildings were transferred almost overnight to Laramie.

Although the rails moved swiftly on west of Laramie, the town went through a wild period, its violence intensified because of vigilante efforts to halt the general lawlessness. After the town's business leaders lynched a desperado known as 'The Kid', a gun battle broke out in Belle of the West, one of the dingier dance halls. Five men were killed, fifteen wounded; the determined vigilantes captured four outlaws and hanged them from telegraph poles alongside the UP station. When a newspaper correspondent arrived shortly afterwards to report the incident, he was told that the hanged men had broken their necks while climbing the telegraph poles. By this time, another end-of-track town, Benton, was ready for a westward shift of the Hell on Wheels, and most of the gamblers, saloonkeepers, and outlaws began leaving Laramie.

In the meantime, Durant and Seymour had aroused the anger of Casement and Reed by ordering them to make a change in Dodge's original survey. To avoid extensive grading and filling across the rough country between Laramie City and the Laramie plains, Seymour recommended a new route through the valleys of Rock Creek and Medicine Bow River. This change would add twenty miles to the railroad, but it could be speedily constructed and would bring almost two million easy dollars into the pockets of the railroad's builders. At this time, Dodge was in Washington serving as congressman from the Iowa district of which he claimed to be a resident. Most of his efforts were directed towards legislation favouring the Union Pacific, and he still held his title of chief engineer of the railroad. Early in May, Dodge received a telegram from Sam Reed informing him of Seymour's and Durant's interference. Dodge immediately packed his bags. He had chosen Cheyenne as a division point because that city was the most logical place for a junction with the railroad from Denver, and he was determined to block Durant's efforts to change it to Laramie. As for Seymour's new survey, Dodge viewed it as being as crooked as was its originator. Just as his predecessor, Peter Dey, had rebelled as the result of Seymour's interference in lengthening the road out of Omaha three years earlier, Dodge's professionalism could not accept the proposed change. Instead of resigning as Dey had done, however, he telegraphed President Oliver Ames of the UP, secured his support, and then boarded a train for Wyoming, determined to have a showdown.

When Dodge arrived at Cheyenne, he learned that Durant had already ordered the repair shops moved to Laramie and that grading had begun on Seymour's winding route to the Laramie plains. Dodge countermanded Durant's order concerning the railroad shops, and then had his private car hitched to a locomotive for a fast run to Laramie. There, by chance, he met Durant walking on a street crowded with the usual gambling establishments. According to Dodge, it was not a cordial meeting. He informed

Durant that he was still chief engineer of the UP and that he could not tolerate any interference in engineering matters. 'The men working for the Union Pacific will take orders from me and not from you,' Dodge quoted himself as saying. 'If you interfere there will be trouble – trouble from the government, from the Army, and from the men themselves.' Durant was well aware of Dodge's excellent governmental and military connections. He made no reply as Dodge turned and strode back towards the Laramie station.

Grading and filling was now too far along on Seymour's route to make a change, but as soon as the track layers reached the Laramie plains, Jack Casement set a goal of two miles a day, offering extra pay to men willing to work on moonlit nights and on Sundays. The Casements' new contract stipulated payment to them of eight hundred dollars per mile for less than two miles laid in a day, twelve hundred dollars a mile for over two miles a day. During that summer, the UP and its contractors had ten thousand men strung out across Wyoming and into northeastern Utah. After three years of trial and error, Sam Reed, the Casement brothers, and their assistants had achieved a high degree of efficiency in planning and in organization. They had learned that forty carloads of supplies were required to build each mile of track, and discovered the importance of time-and-motion studies before that technique was given a name. Even so, the pressures upon the graders to keep ahead of the track layers resulted in what one government examiner described as 'very hastily and inefficiently made up' earthen fills. After travelling over one such section, President Oliver Ames admitted that the grades and curves would have to be improved as soon as the road was completed, 'though it will be a heavy additional cost'.

At Mary's Creek, the UP had to build its first tunnel through a rugged spur of sandstone that blocked a gorge along which the tracks were to run. To avoid a delay in track construction, the resourceful Casements bypassed the spur, laying miles of rails ahead of the tunnelling crew.

In the heat of July, the UP was plotting another town, which somebody ironically decided to name for Senator Thomas Hart Benton. The late senator had spent years advocating a transcontinental railroad along the 38th parallel, and now here was his town almost astride the predestined 42nd parallel. Nearby, General Sherman's Army was building Fort Fred Steele, and Dr Durant's promoters used its presence to create an air of permanence about the city of Benton and to boost the price of lots. Although the streets were filled with burning alkali dust, and water had to be hauled three miles in wagons from the North Platte River for a dollar per barrel, the lots were eagerly and quickly bought up. Two months later, Benton was a ghost town, with nothing left there but a sidetrack for the use and convenience of the fort.

During its Hell on Wheels heyday, however, Benton had twenty-three saloons and five dance halls. Twice each day, long freight trains arrived from the East to unload tons of goods for reshipment by wagons to all points west. 'For ten hours daily the streets were thronged with motley crowds of railroadmen, Mexicans and Indians, gamblers, "cappers", saloonkeepers, merchants, miners and mulewhackers,' wrote newspaper correspondent John Hanson Beadle. 'The streets were eight inches deep in white dust as I entered the city of canvas tents and polehouses; the suburbs appeared as banks of dirty white lime, and a new arrival with black clothes looked like nothing so much as a cockroach struggling through a flour barrel ... The great institution of Benton was the "Big Tent". This structure was a nice frame, a hundred feet long and forty feet wide, covered with canvas and conveniently floored for dancing, to which and gambling it was entirely devoted.'

Publisher Samuel Bowles found Benton disgusting by day, dangerous by night, 'a congregation of scum and wickedness ... almost everybody dirty, many filthy, and with the marks of lowest vice; averaging a murder a day; gambling and drinking, hurdy-gurdy dancing and the vilest of sexual commerce, the chief business and pastime of the hours, – this was Benton. Like its predecessors, it fairly festered in corruption, disorder and death, and would have rotted, even in this dry air, had it outlasted a brief sixty-day life. But in a few weeks its tents were struck, its shanties razed, and with their dwellers moved on fifty or a hundred miles farther to repeat their life for another brief day. Where these people came from originally; where they went to when the road was finished, and their occupation over, were both puzzles too intricate for me. Hell would appear to have been raked to furnish them; and to it they must have naturally returned after graduating here, fitted for its highest seats and most diabolical service.'

Before Benton died, some of the tents were replaced with pre-fabricated buildings that had been shipped all the way from Chicago. In a dim light, a passerby would swear that they were built of brick and brownstone, but actually they were merely boards painted to simulate more permanent materials. 'The meanest place I have ever been in,' was the way Jack Casement described Benton in a letter to his wife, but Casement was irri-tated by the August heat, which was slowing construction, and Utah was still miles and miles beyond the western horizon. Case-ment was also annoyed by a constant succession of excursionists brought out by Durant and Seymour to encourage sales of rail-road stock. According to Casement, one excursion party con-tained 'all the Professors of Yale College and a lot of Rail Road men with their ladies ... a great nuisance to the work.'

The most important excursion party of the summer was that of General Ulysses Grant, who as the candidate of the Republican party was campaigning for the office of President of the United States. Somewhat in the manner of modern candidates who visit foreign lands to demonstrate their breadth of vision, Grant was travelling across the West to demonstrate his interest in the transcontinental railroad and what was then called 'the Indian Problem'. Late in July he arrived at Laramie City in company with a touring party of eight generals among whom were Sher-man and Sheridan. By this time Durant had managed to secure from the executive committee of the Union Pacific a resolution that gave him authority to direct construction operations in the field. Armed with this weapon, Durant managed to see Grant and ask his support in removing Dodge as chief engineer. Grant re-fused to commit himself until he heard Dodge's side of the feud; consequently, a telegram had to be sent to Dodge, who was in-specting the Mormons' grading work in Utah, requesting his presence at Fort Sanders for a conference with Grant, Durant, Dillon, and Seymour.

Politics was a complicating intruder at this meeting. Silas Seymour's brother, Horatio Seymour, was the Democratic candidate for President, running in opposition to Grant. If Horatio Seymour should win, Durant through his connections with Silas would gain direct access to presidential powers and decisions. But only the most fanatical partisans believed that anyone could defeat Grant, the military hero of the reunited nation. And with Grant in office, his wartime comrade Dodge certainly would be the Union Pacific's man of influence with the presidency.

The confrontation occurred on 26 July 1868, in an ornately constructed log cabin used as the officers' club at Fort Sanders. Grant, Sherman, and Sheridan wore civilian clothing. Dodge, lean and sunburned, arrived wearing an engineer's cap, his boots polished to a high shine. Durant's pasty face was determined; he wore loose black summer corduroys, a gold watch chain pendant across his vest. Dillon, of Credit Mobilier, in a dark coat and grey trousers, could have been an actor cast in the role of a capitalist giant. Seymour, his hair and beard neatly trimmed as usual, kept to the background.

If we may believe Dodge's account, Grant opened the proceedings by commenting in his dry fashion upon the Army's difficulties in pacifying hostile Indians so as to keep them from attacking the railroad's graders and track layers. Having spent so much money and effort at this, he said, the government had the right to expect peaceable relations among the builders of the road.

Durant plunged immediately to the attack, charging Dodge with having wasted money upon preliminary surveys, with having chosen routes too costly to construct, with ignoring the advice of his associates, and with angering the Mormons by routing the line north of Salt Lake. After Durant finished, Grant glanced at Dodge.

'If Durant, or anybody connected with the Union Pacific, or anybody connected with the government changes my lines,' Dodge said calmly, 'I'll quit the road.'

Nobody spoke for a few moments, and then Grant broke the silence: 'The government expects the railroad company to meet its obligations. And the government expects General Dodge to remain with the road as its chief engineer until it is completed.'

Durant was a realist. He knew that within a few months, barring a miracle, the man who had directed those words to him would be President of the United States. Hesitating only a moment, Durant turned towards Dodge. 'I withdraw my objections,' he said. 'We all want Dodge to stay with the road.'

That of course was Dodge's story. No one else present appears to have made any record of this second showdown with Durant.

Dodge returned to Utah, and while the UP track layers endured the heat and desolation of Wyoming's Red Desert, he sought out his opposite number on the Central Pacific, chief engineer Samuel Montague. With his usual bluntness, Dodge told Montague that UP tracks would be in Ogden by the spring of 1869. To save time and money, he suggested, the two railroads should decide upon a definite meeting place somewhere west of Ogden. Montague, however, declined to name a specific place. The Great Race, with all its wastefulness, would still continue.

As the summer waned, swarms of newspapermen arrived daily from the East, dispatching bulletins 'from the front' much in the manner of war correspondents. They reported each day's progress in miles and quarter miles of track laid towards the Wasatch Mountain barrier of Utah. 'Sherman with his victorious legions sweeping from Atlanta to Savannah was a spectacle less glorious than this army of men marching on foot from Omaha to Sacramento, subduing unknown wildernesses, scaling unknown mountains, surmounting untried obstacles, and binding across the broad breast of America the iron emblem of modern progress and civilization.'

Late in October the track layers were within a few miles of the Utah line, but each night ice rimmed the tops of the water barrels, warning that winter would come early in the mountains. In November they reached Bear River; this was the heart of the old fur-trade country of Jim Bridger and the Mountain Men. The rugged fur trappers, accustomed to the wild excitements of their annual rendezvous, would have felt right at home in Bear River City, but even they might have been astonished by the riot of 19 November when a gang of outlaws who had been driven out of town by vigilantes returned in force to burn the town's jail and sack the office of the *Frontier Index*, the peripatetic newspaper that had followed the railroad west from Fort Kearney,

Nebraska. Opinions differed as to whether the outlaws destroyed the newspaper because they believed the editor was the leader of the vigilantes or because he was a Seymour Democrat who had used his editorial columns to attack Ulysses S. Grant as a 'whisky bloated, squaw ravishing, adulterous, monkey ridden, nigger worshipping mogul.' At any rate, Bear River City died not long after that, and a traveller who passed through a year later said that there was nothing left to mark the place 'except a few posts and old chimneys, broken bottles and shattered oyster cans'.

December snows began to plague the graders and track layers after they crossed into Utah, and each day the gang foremen expected to receive orders to make winter camp. But there was to be no work stoppage in the winter of 1868–9. Alarmed by the rapid progress of the CP across the Nevada deserts, and greedy for the mile subsidies and land grants that might be lost to the Big Four across Utah, Durant persuaded the UP directors to order full speed ahead through the Wasatch Range. Now the UP workmen would have to endure the same hardships suffered by CP workmen in the Sierras. They dragged timber out of snowbanks, moved frozen earth with picks and shovels, laid tracks on icy crusts, and learned by experience how to blast tunnels through the red sandstone of Echo and Weber canyons.

Being as eager as Durant to beat the CP into Ogden, Dodge did not resist Durant's orders, but he admitted that laying the track in snow and ice was done at tremendous cost, over ten million dollars he estimated. The head of the railroad's freight department complained that the track west of Bear River was 'not fit to run over and we are ditching trains daily', and on one of Dodge's inspection tours he saw a train slide off a collapsing embankment and overturn. One of the few newspaper reporters hardy enough to stay in the field reported that tracks were laid on snow and ice, which then melted or evaporated, leaving ties and rails dangling in the air. Entire grades, he said, were so soft that the weight of trains would cause them to slide into rivers below. Accidents and fatalities increased rapidly, but when the men complained, their foremen used the old anti-Chinese prejudices to keep the Great Race from slowing down. Were the tarriers of the UP going to let the little yellow Chinamen beat them into Ogden? Never! Jack Casement found plenty of track layers willing to work after sundown by lanternlight in bitter cold.

They celebrated Christmas Day by bringing the end of track into Wahsatch, only sixty-seven miles from Ogden. Durant was there in his comfortable private car for the celebration, but snow was piled high along the tracks and correspondent John H. Beadle reported that the temperature in the dining room of the town's only hotel was five degrees below zero. 'A drop of the hottest coffee spilled upon the cloth froze in a minute, while the gravy was hard on the plate, and the butter frozen in spite of the fastest eater.' Twenty-eight-year-old John Beadle was a graduate of Michigan State, a Civil War veteran from Indiana, who had come to the West expecting to die from an ailment diagnosed as consumption, but he made a miraculous recovery during his zestful pursuit of news stories about the railroad for the *Cincinnati Commercial.*

When Jack Casement informed Durant that some of his men were near the breaking point, Durant told him to double the wages and keep the work going. Doubling the wages, however, meant little to the workmen, because they were already several weeks behind in receiving their pay. During Christmas week, Credit Mobilier had poured out its fifth bountiful dividend of 1868 to its tight little ring of stockholders (several of whom were congressmen) leaving the Union Pacific Railroad Company six million dollars in debt and with no funds to pay contractors and workmen. To add to the difficulties, government inspectors were refusing to certify some of the recent construction, holding up expected subsidies. In New York, Jim Fisk, a former Yankee peddler of silk goods who had become a notorious financial speculator and manipulator, was threatening an injunction suit against the railroad in a move to gain control of it. Brigham Young was pressing hard for money to pay his Mormon graders, and even the optimistic Jack Casement complained that the company owed him a hundred thousand dollars. 'The banks are loaded with UPRR paper,' he said, 'and if The Company don't send some money here soon they will burst up the whole country.'

Although Dillon of Credit Mobilier was as responsible for the railroad's poor financial condition as was Durant, the latter received much of the blame from associates who were aware of the avaricious tendencies of their vice-president and general manager. They knew that Durant and Seymour were silent partners in firms that sold supplies to the railroad at excessive prices, that Durant was receiving ten per cent of many contracts and had instructed construction supervisors to report double the actual quantities of rock hauled for fills, and that Seymour was also receiving kickbacks from tie-cutting contractors and timber haulers. Herbert Hoxie, the Iowa politician who had been a beneficiary of Durant's manipulations in his 1865 contract switch to Credit Mobilier, feared that the sharp practices had gone too far and declared privately that 'the entire outfit was rotten to the core'.

But the UP's worst blow of the winter came when Secretary of the Interior abruptly ordered the railroad to cease construction at Echo Summit, forty miles east of Ogden. When the order reached Utah, the road already had tracks several miles west of Echo Summit and grades were approaching Ogden. The UP's directors were counting on subsidies from the tracks built to Ogden, and probably beyond, to pull them out of their financial squeeze. To halt construction now might mean bankruptcy for the road. Suspecting that wily old Collis Huntington had put pressure on government officials to recognize the Central Pacific's right-of-way maps across Utah, which he had filed with the Department of the Interior, the directors of the Union Pacific decided that politics was involved in the action. They gambled on the fact that Grenville Dodge's good friend, General Grant, would be inaugurated as President within a few weeks and that a new Secretary of the Interior would be in office. And so they boldly ignored the order to stop construction, and pressed on towards Ogden. They also increased their lobbying activities among influential congressmen who were not yet receiving monetary benefits from Credit Mobilier stock.

On the morning of 8 March 1869, four days after Grant became President, Jack Casement's track gangs laid rails into Ogden, and that afternoon an Iron Horse rolled in, its whistle drowning the music of a welcoming brass band. Dodge and Reed were there to celebrate not only the railroad's capture of Ogden, but also news just received that in his first cabinet meeting President

Grant had cancelled the order to halt Union Pacific construction at Echo Summit.

As soon as the celebration ended, Casement had his track layers back at work, and a month later they were at Corinne. This town would be the next to the last of tent-and-tarpaper grading camps that the arrival of rails converted to the usual roaring den of sin. A land agent for the UP named the town for his daughter (an act that he must have later regretted) and he promoted Corinne as Utah's future non-Mormon city, the 'Chicago of the Rocky Mountains'. A few weeks later when Charles Savage arrived to photograph the booming town, he said that all of Corinne was 'on the wrong side of the tracks'. For a time John Beadle ran a newspaper there and boasted that 'the town contained eighty *nymphs du pavé*, popularly known in Mountain-English as "soiled doves" ... Yet it was withal a quiet and rather orderly place. Sunday was generally observed: most of the men went hunting or fishing, and the "girls" had a dance, or got drunk.'

Only fifty miles now separated contenders in the Great Race, and it was obvious that they must meet somewhere in the Promontory Range. Yet, no effort was being made by the leaders of either side to choose a specific meeting place. Like two weary but evenly matched armies at the end of a long war, each railroad company continued to manoeuvre for advantages over the other, running their parallel grades for miles past each other, the CP stubbornly heading for Ogden, and the UP hellbent for nowhere. Notable examples of waste were the UP's Big Trestle and the CP's Big Fill, both of which crossed the same deep gorge within 150 feet of each other. The CP used 500 men and 250 teams in hauling earth during most of February and March 1869, to build the embankment across the canyon. When the UP reached the same point, Seymour refused to waste time on a fill and ordered Sam Reed to construct a trestle. A newspaper reporter was appalled by the flimsy structure. 'The cross pieces are jointed in the most clumsy manner,' he wrote. 'The Central Pacific have a fine, solid embankment alongside it, which ought to be used as a track.'

At last President Grant had to intercede. He summoned Grenville Dodge to Washington and asked him to arrange a meeting between representatives of both companies. If they could not decide where their tracks would join, the government would do it for them. As Huntington was in Washington, lobbying as usual, Dodge informed him of what Grant had said, and on 8 April the two men held an all-night meeting. The next morning they telegraphed officials of their respective railroads and informed them of their agreement; after receiving approval from them, they informed Congress that the Union Pacific and the Central Pacific would join their tracks at Promontory Point.

No record was kept of the Dodge-Huntington discussions, but Huntington evidently used the maps he had filed, claiming the route across Utah to Echo Summit, as a weapon to force Dodge to compromise and permit the CP to lease or buy the UP tracks from Promontory to Ogden. Thus did the CP gain what it had set out to achieve, a route into the Great Basin of Utah. In the end, the UP did not do so badly either: the company sold its tracks to the CP for over a million dollars and also pocketed the government subsidies for each of the fifty-three miles from Ogden to Promontory Point.

While these decisive events were occurring in Washington, the rambunctious Jim Fisk stirred up trouble in New York for the Union Pacific by filing a lawsuit on the pretext of protecting his rights as a stockholder. Fisk had smelled out the money bounty of Credit Mobilier, and charged that it was looting the Union Pacific. What Fisk wanted was to throw the railroad into bankruptcy, in the hope that he could gain control of it. He went so far as to form an alliance with the corrupt New York political boss William Marcy Tweed, and staged a raid on the Union Pacific offices to seize company records. President Oliver Ames, however, managed to transfer the books to New Jersey, out of Tweed's jurisdiction, thereby keeping the lid on Credit Mobilier's relations with the railroad – until another day. Jim Fisk had touched a sensitive nerve in the closely related financial-political establishment of America, but his reputation was so unsavoury that he gained no supporters among the few honest men in Congress, who were also beginning to suspect that something was amiss in the financing of the people's railroad to the Western Sea. And so the entire affair evaporated in the atmosphere of exhilaration with which the young republic awaited the approaching day when the Great Race would end at Promontory Point.

There was one more event to be staged for the benefit of newspapermen and photographers who were gathering in that last of the railroad boom towns, Promontory City, which consisted of one long street of tents and false-fronted wooden structures set back only a few yards from the railroad track. According to rumour, Charlie Crocker had once boasted to Dr Durant that his CP workmen could lay ten miles of track in a single day, whereupon Durant had bet Crocker ten thousand dollars that such a feat could never be accomplished. At any rate, as the two railroads approached each other at Promontory Point, Crocker announced that 28 April would be Ten-Mile Day.

For the railroad workmen this event was of greater importance than was the final joining of the rails, and both companies declared a holiday for all except the few hundred men engaged in the great undertaking. After distributing ties along the grade, Crocker and Strobridge planned everything like a military operation, bringing up carloads of rails, fishplates, bolts, and spikes at regular intervals, using Chinese on handcars pulled by horses to move the iron forward to the gaugers, spikers, bolters, and a picked crew of eight rail carriers. These eight iron men were of course the sporting heroes of the day, and their names – Sullivan, Dailey, Kennedy, Joyce, Shay, Eliott, Killeen, McNamara – reveal their ancestry. Every participant moved at full speed, jumping, trotting, running, dancing, pausing only occasionally to take a sip of water or tea from pails that a detachment of constantly moving Chinese carried on poles over their shoulders.

By one-thirty they had laid six miles of rails, and Crocker ordered a stop for lunch. He offered to release any track layer who had had enough. Nobody accepted the offer. An hour later they were back at work. At seven o'clock, James Strobridge signalled victory. In twelve hours, a full working day, they were fifty-six feet past the ten-mile mark. During that day, someone later calculated, the track layers had spiked 3,520 rails to 25,800 ties, and each rail handler had lifted 250,000 pounds of iron.

Although Dr Durant was not there to witness the loss of his ten-thousand-dollar bet, Grenville Dodge was among the spectators. 'I saw them lay their special ten miles on that wager,' he commented, 'but they were a week preparing for it, and bedded all their ties beforehand.' For him it was only a stunt. The joining of the rails and the driving of the last spike would be the day of accomplishment.

Promontory Point, Promontory Summit, Promontory Station – all these names were used – lay in a waterless basin of sagebrush, ringed on three sides by mountains. Tracks of the Central Pacific reached there on 30 April, and the Californians had to wait a week before the Union Pacific track layers came into view. On 1 May, hundreds of men lined up at the paymasters' cars of both railroads to receive their last wages, and thousands of others learned that they would work only one more week. 'The two opposing armies,' reported a newspaper correspondent, 'are melting away.' The Great Race was coming to an end.

Only twenty-five hundred feet of empty grading lay between the two railroads on 7 May, but that afternoon, when Leland Stanford's special train arrived for the planned celebration of 8 May, Jack Casement came over to inform the Central Pacific's president and several accompanying dignitaries that the joining of the rails would have to be delayed until 10 May. According to Casement, heavy rains had washed out part of the UP tracks in Weber Canyon, and the special train carrying Durant, Dillon, and other officials could not move until repairs were completed.

But there was more to the story than that. On 6 May, when the UP special pulled into Piedmont, Wyoming, from the East, an armed mob of several hundred railroad workmen surrounded Durant's private car, switched it onto a sidetrack, and chained the wheels to the rails. Spokesmen for the workers informed the startled Dr Durant that he and his very important associates were prisoners until the men received their overdue wages. The amount demanded remains obscure because Union Pacific officials then and afterwards maintained great secrecy about the incident, but various contemporary accounts gave estimates varying from $12,000 to $80,000 to $235,000. Some historians suspect that Mormons were leaders in this affair, as the railroad had repeatedly ignored Brigham Young's demands for payment of his grading contract. Although attempts were made to effect Durant's rescue by summoning soldiers from nearby Army posts, all telegrams to

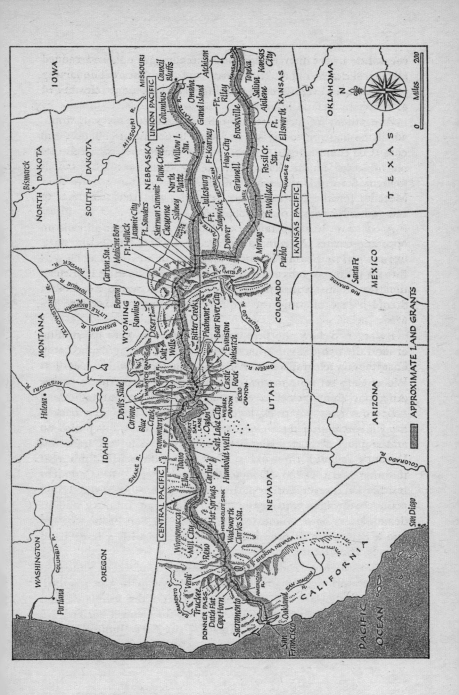

the military were intercepted, and he finally gave up and arranged for payroll funds to be telegraphed from New York headquarters.

While these events were occurring, Jack Casement felt obliged to entertain Leland Stanford and his friends from California by inviting them for a sightseeing ride to Ogden on his work train, which he had previously stocked with 'a bountiful collation and oceans of champagne'. As the weather was dismal with rain, no one objected to the delay, and during their overnight stay in Ogden, Stanford and some of the other orators wrote their speeches for the forthcoming ceremonies and released them to the gathering swarm of newspapermen.

A cold rain was still falling on Sunday 9 May, but all rails on both approaches to Promontory, except the final connecting ones, were spiked to the ties. The next morning the weather had cleared into an ideal day for celebration, white clouds floating in a clean blue sky against a distant backdrop of cedar-covered mountains, a cool breeze blowing, the temperature rising to sixty-nine degrees.

By seven o'clock the first curious spectators were assembling around the two-rail gap where a huge American flag flapped atop an adjoining telegraph pole. Alongside the grade, whisky peddlers had already set up tents to sell refreshments at premium prices. At about eight o'clock a construction train arrived to unload boisterous gangs of track layers and graders, and then backed away. Shortly after ten o'clock, two Union Pacific trains pulled up and stopped a short distance from the gap. The first train was Durant's delayed three-car special, and riding with him that morning were Dillon, Dodge, Seymour, Reed, the Casement brothers, and several other officials and guests. Aboard the second train were four companies of the Twenty-first Infantry and its headquarters band bound for the Presidio at San Francisco, and also a delegation of prominent Utah citizens with a brass band from Salt Lake City.

While these arrivals were detraining, a gang of blue-clad Chinese workmen began levelling up the gap in the roadbed. They laid the last ties and rails, bolted on the fishplates, and drove all but the last few spikes. At 11.15 the Central Pacific train puffed into view. Both Iron Horses – the CP's 'Jupiter' with a

flared funnel stack and the UP's No. 119 with a straight cylindrical stack capped by a spark-arrester – were now uncoupled and
brought into facing positions across the meeting place of the
rails. The soldiers of the Twenty-first Infantry formed a double
line facing the tracks and stood at parade rest.

By this time Stanford and the members of his party were shaking hands with the Union Pacific officials, and they began dis-
cussing the agenda of the ceremonies. Stanford had brought
along two golden spikes, a silver spike, a combination iron, silver,
and gold spike, a silver-plated sledgehammer, and a polished
laurel tie, but very little planning had been done in regard to
protocol. Dr Durant, clad in a stylish black velvet jacket, and
suffering from a severe headache probably brought on by excessive consumption of champagne, wished only to get done with the
spike ceremony as quickly as possible, but Grenville Dodge evidently took offence at Stanford's elaborate trappings and insisted
on having a simple ceremony in which *he* would drive the last
spike, an iron one. Even to the very last hour, the rivalry of the
Great Race would not die. It was 11.55, only five minutes before
the scheduled time for beginning the ceremony, when Durant
overruled Dodge and agreed to follow Stanford's programme.

None of those present who recorded the events of the day
agreed on the number of people gathered there. Estimates ranged
from five hundred to three thousand, but judging from the photographs, the total probably was between six and seven hundred,
including the understrength companies of the Twenty-first Infantry, about twenty reporters and photographers, and twenty-
one women, most of whom were wives of railroad officials and
Army officers. 'It was not a large crowd,' Sidney Dillon recalled.
'In brass bands, fireworks, procession and oratory, the demonstra-
tion when ground was broken at Omaha, less than five years before, was much more imposing.' But it should be remembered
that in May 1869, Promontory Point was remote and difficult to
reach. Virtually all of America was there in spirit that day, awaiting eagerly the telegraphic flashes that would signal the symbolic
union of the continent by iron rails.

To speed this communication, a wire had been run from a telegraph pole down to a key on a small table facing the rail gap. At

12.20, telegraph operator W. N. Shilling tapped out a message to Western Union announcing that in about twenty minutes the last spike would be driven. Operators across the nation immediately began clearing their lines. While Shilling's key still chattered, James Strobridge and Sam Reed brought up the laurel tie (in which spike holes had previously been drilled) and placed it in position. The bibulous spectators pressed in so close that Jack Casement had to order them back so that photographers could set up their cameras to record the scene. 'As it was,' reported John Beadle, 'the crowd pushed upon the workmen so closely that less than twenty persons saw the affair entirely, while none of the reporters were able to hear all that was said.' Because of the boisterous jostling and shouting, only those pressed into the inner ring knew that the Reverend John Todd, who was there as a correspondent for two religious magazines, was offering a prayer. They removed their hats, while Dr Todd's voice was drowned in the outer babble of celebrants. He kept the prayer mercifully short, and at 12.40, telegrapher Shilling tapped out: 'We have got done praying. The spike is about to be presented.'

Durant, his head throbbing, pushed forward to accept the two gold spikes from a representative of the Central Pacific. He kneeled and slid them into the prepared holes in the laurel tie, his eyes blinking at the inscribed silver plate: THE LAST TIE LAID ON THE COMPLETION OF THE PACIFIC RAILROAD, MAY 1869. As he arose, Stanford began speaking in the bright sunlight, his voice strong at the end: 'Now, gentlemen, with your assistance we will proceed to lay the last tie, the last rail, and drive the last spike.'

Grenville Dodge made the response: 'Gentlemen, the great Benton proposed that some day a giant statue of Columbus be erected on the highest peak of the Rocky Mountains, pointing westward, denoting that as the great route across the continent. You have made that prophecy today a fact. This is the way to India.'

While the crowd cheered and the bands played, the other spikes and the silver-headed sledgehammer were brought forward. After a telegraph wire was attached to the last spike, Stanford raised the sledge and brought it down briskly, missing the spike entirely. The inebriated track layers roared with laughter. Durant put on a pair of gauntlets to protect his tender palms, lifted the sledge, and also missed. Aware that the blows of the sledgehammer had not gone out over the wire, telegrapher Shilling touched his key and tapped out: 'Done'. The time was 12.47, 2.47 on the Eastern seaboard. 'We all yelled like to bust,' was the way one of the spectators described it.

After the gold and silver spikes and the laurel tie were carefully removed, the CP's 'Jupiter' and the UP's No. 119 eased forward until their pilots clanged together. While cheering workmen climbed up onto both Iron Horses, their engineers scrambled to the boiler fronts with bottles of champagne, to shake hands and exchange toasts. The photographers worked frantically to clear the crowd back so that the railroad's chief engineers, Grenville Dodge and Samuel Montague, could stand before the two locomotives in another symbolic handclasp.

As soon as the wet-plate photographs were made, the 'Jupiter' reversed its wheels and made room for No. 119 to cross the rail junction. Then No. 119 backed up, and the 'Jupiter' with a merry whistle blast eased across to the UP's tracks. The transcontinental railroad was ready for the Iron Horses to roll.

Somewhat reluctantly, the workmen who had made it all possible (most of whom were now unemployed) drifted away to the whisky tents and dance halls of Promontory City. The well-dressed owners of the railroads gathered in Dr Durant's private car for more champagne toasts. In all the cities of America, bells were ringing, flags were flying, whistles were blowing, cannons were firing, people were singing, and orators were declaiming: 'The Anglo-Saxon and the Celt met in friendly greeting the tawny Asiatic at Promontory Point, and rejoiced together over the final consummation of the enterprise which their united labors have achieved ... California shook hands with New York and New England, and the mingled screams of steam whistles upon engines waked the echoes of the mountains.'

In Chicago, an impromptu parade seven miles long jammed the streets of the city. In New York, a hundred guns fired salutes in City Hall Park, and Wall Street suspended business for the day. In Philadelphia, flags were hoisted everywhere and the pealing of bells on Independence Hall set off the music of church bells all across the city. In Buffalo, the populace poured into the streets to sing 'The Star Spangled Banner' and fire engines assembled to blow whistles in concert. In Sacramento, thirty Iron Horses gaily bedecked and drawn up into line screeched out a concert of joy. In San Francisco, the celebration became a bedlam that lasted well into the night, and that city's leading man of letters, Bret Harte, sat down to compose a poem:

What was it the Engines said,
Pilots touching – head to head
Facing on the single track,
Half a world behind each back?
This is what the Engines said,
Unreported and unread.

With a prefatory screech,
In a florid Western speech,
Said the Engine from the West:
'I am from Sierra's crest;
And if altitude's a test,
Why, I reckon, it's confessed
That I've done my level best.'

Said the Engine from the East:
'They who work best talk the least.
S'pose you whistle down your brakes;
What you've done is no great shakes,
Pretty fair, – but let our meeting
Be a different kind of greeting.
Let these folks with champagne stuffing,
Not their Engines, do the *puffing*.

'Listen! Where Atlantic beats
Shores of snow and summer heats;
Where the Indian and summer skies
Paint the woods with wampum dyes, –
I have chased the flying sun,
Seeing all he looked upon,
Blessing all that he has blessed,
Nursing in my iron breast
All his vivifying heat,
All his clouds about my crest;
And before my flying feet
Every shadow must retreat.'

Said the Western Engine, 'Phew!'
And a long, low whistle blew,
'Come, now, really that's the oddest
Talk for one so very modest.
You brag of your East! *You* do?
Why, *I* bring the East to *you*!
All the Orient, all Cathay,
Find through me the shortest way;
And the sun you follow here
Rises in my hemisphere.
Really, – if one must be rude, –
Length, my friend, ain't longitude.'

Said the Union: 'Don't reflect, or
I'll run over some Director.'
Said the Central: 'I'm Pacific;
But, when riled, I'm quite terrific.
Yet today we shall not quarrel,
Just to show these folks this moral,
How two Engines – their vision –
Once have met without collision.'

That is what the Engines said,
Unreported and unread;
Spoken slightly through the nose,
With a whistle at the close.

SEVEN

First Travellers on the Transcontinental

I see over my own continent the Pacific railroad
  surmounting every barrier,
I see continual trains of cars winding along
  the Platte carrying freight and passengers,
I hear the locomotives rushing and roaring,
  and the shrill steamwhistle,
I hear the echoes reverberate through the
  grandest scenery in the world ...

Bridging the three or four thousand miles
  of land travel,
Tying the Eastern to the Western sea ...

WHITMAN, *Passage to India*

On 15 May 1869, regular train service began on America's first
transcontinental railroad. Thousands of Americans who had become accustomed to train travel in the Eastern states could now
journey behind an Iron Horse all the way to Walt Whitman's
Western Sea. Although it was not possible – except in cases of
special excursions – to board a car in an Eastern city and journey
uninterrupted to California, most of these pioneer travellers
seemed to look upon the necessary transfers in Chicago and
Omaha, and Promontory or Ogden, as welcome breaks in an
eight- to ten-day adventure.

'Every man who could command the time and money was
eager to make the trip,' declared that energetic travelling reporter John Beadle, 'and everybody who could sling ink became
correspondents.' From the very beginning, many travellers did
indeed seem compelled to make written records of their experi-
ences. Their accounts were usually very sketchy until they passed

Chicago or Omaha. During the first year of transcontinental service, passengers from the East arrived in Chicago on the Michigan Central Railroad, but by the mid-1870s they had their choice of connections from the Pennsylvania, Erie, or New York Central.

'Seventy-five minutes are allowed for getting from the station of arrival to the station of departure,' said William F. Rae, an Englishman who made the journey late in 1869. 'In my own case the times of the trains did not correspond; the one train had started an hour before the other arrived.' Because he had planned to stop over briefly in Chicago, Rae was not disappointed by the enforced delay of twenty-four hours, but many of his fellow passengers were, and for another century travellers through Chicago would continue to suffer the inconvenience of changing trains and failure to make connections. During the heyday of American railroad passenger travel, one of the common sayings was that a hog could travel across country through Chicago without changing cars, but a human being could not.

To reach the Union Pacific from Chicago, travellers had their choice of two direct routes, the Rock Island or the Northwestern, and an indirect route, the Chicago, Burlington & Quincy. Knowledgeable people taking the direct routes soon learned to avoid the evening express trains, which left them stranded in Council Bluffs or Omaha for almost twenty-four hours while they awaited the departure of the UP's daily train for the Pacific Coast.

Until a bridge was completed across the Missouri River in 1872, western travellers also had to endure a crossing 'in a rickety old ferry boat' from Council Bluffs to Omaha. 'On arriving at Council Bluffs,' reported William Rae, 'we found omnibuses in waiting at the station. The morning was cold and raw. But a small proportion of the passengers could get inside seats, the remainder having the option of either sitting on the roof among the luggage or else being left behind. In itself the seat on the roof was not objectionable, provided the time occupied was brief. As nearly an hour was thus spent, the feeling of satisfaction at having got a seat at all was supplanted by a feeling of annoyance at the treatment received. Through deep ruts in the mud the omnibus was slowly drawn by four horses to the river's bank, and thence on to the deck of a flat-bottomed steamer. Seated there, a good view was had of the Missouri. It has been called mighty, which it doubtless is considered as a stream, yet the appellation of "Big Muddy", which is current here, is the one which more truthfully characterizes it.'

And then after the bridge was built, the railroads refused to be cooperative enough to take the cars of the Eastern roads across the river to the Union Pacific station. Arriving in Council Bluffs, passengers had to remove themselves and their baggage to the cars of the Transfer Company, 'whose province is to put passengers to all sorts of inconvenience and trouble in crossing over the river.' John Erastus Lester of Providence, Rhode Island, who travelled West in 1872 in the hope of improving his health, said that passage by the Transfer Company 'caused more hard words to be spoken than can be erased from the *big book* for many a day'. He was not only disenchanted by the company's treatment of passengers but by its requirement that all freight be unloaded from Eastern cars and then repacked for shipment across the river.

Early travellers on the transcontinental railroad saw little to admire about Omaha. One found it to be 'the muddiest place I ever saw,' but added that 'the roads are generally deep with dust.' Another also described the town as being layered with mud through which 'the omnibus laboured slowly, the outside passengers being advised by the driver to move about from one side of the roof to another, in order to guard against upsetting the overloaded vehicle. A general feeling of relief was manifested when the station of the Union Pacific Railway was reached.'

Almost all agreed that they had seldom seen such bustling confusion as that which developed at the Omaha station at the times for train departures. During the early years when the journey to the West was considered a daring enterprise, rumours were deliberately spread among the greenhorn ticket buyers of the possibility that wild Indians would attack or wreck the trains; this of course aided the Omaha railroad agents in the sale of insurance policies for the journey.

Except for a quick whistle from the engine and the conductor's cry of 'All aboard!' there was no warning of the train's departure. This usually resulted in a rush of passengers who had to hop on board the moving cars. 'For three or four miles we pass along the bluffs on which Omaha is built,' John Lester recorded, 'and then push out upon the open prairie, the fertile lands of Nebraska. A vast plain, dotted here and there with trees, stretches away upon every side.'

In springtime, the rolling land was covered with wild flowers whose fragrance drifted into the open windows of cars moving along at twenty miles an hour; in summer, tumbleweeds by the thousands wheeled across the drying grass; and by autumn, prairie fires blazed against the horizon. 'The spectacle of a prairie on fire is one of infinite grandeur,' said William Rae. 'For miles on every side the air is heavy with volumes of stifling smoke, and the ground reddened with hissing and rushing fire.'

Travellers from abroad found the Great Plains grass shorter than they had expected, and they compared the wind-driven sweep of greyish green to ocean waves, 'undulating like the Atlantic with a heavy groundswell'. They also complained of their eyes wearying at the sameness of landscape, of the train seeming to be standing still in an immense void. All welcomed the first break in the montony of the plains – the Platte River, which the railroad followed westward as had the wagon trains of earlier years.

When the transcontinental railroad opened for service, George Mortimer Pullman had been manufacturing experimental models of his sleeping cars for four years, and the Union Pacific accepted several of them in 1869. They were called Pullman Palace cars and their exteriors were painted in rich brown colours to distinguish them from the drab coaches. Everyone who could afford the additional twenty-five dollars for first-class fare and four dollars per day for a Pullman Palace car was eager to obtain a berth. First-class travellers paid one hundred dollars for the journey from Omaha to Sacramento; second-class or coach, seventy-five dollars. There was also a special rate of forty dollars for immigrants, who rode on cramped board seats. Four to five days were usually required to complete the journey by express, six to seven days by mixed train. The speed of trains varied according to the conditions of tracks and bridges, dropping to nine miles per hour over hastily built sections and increasing to thirty-five miles per hour over smoother tracks. Most travellers of the early 1870s mentioned eighteen to twenty-two miles per hour as the average. Although speeds were doubled within a decade, time-consuming stops and starts at more than two hundred stations and water tanks prevented any considerable reduction in total hours spent on the long journey.

Even in an era when the most highly skilled Americans earned less than a hundred dollars a month, demand for hundred-dollar Pullman space on the transcontinental railroad was so great that early in 1870 the Union Pacific began running three sleeping cars on some trains and still had to turn away would-be ticket buyers. Because of George Pullman's interest in the Union Pacific, he supplied that railroad with deluxe innovations long before they reached the Eastern roads. Travellers heard or read about the Palace cars and were eager to ride on them no matter what the cost. 'I had a sofa to myself, with a table and a lamp,' wrote one satisfied rider. 'The sofas are widened and made into beds at night. My berth was three feet three inches wide, and six feet three inches long. It had two windows looking out of the train, a handsome mirror, and was well furnished with bedding and curtains.'

British travellers were especially impressed, and sent off earnest letters to railway directors in London, urging them 'to take a leaf out of the Americans' book, and provide sleeping carriages for long night journeys.' They also delighted in the freedom of movement from one car to another, although the traveller who signed himself 'A London Parson' admitted that trying to dress oneself in a box two feet high was a bit inconvenient. 'It was an odd experience, that going to bed of some thirty ladies, gentlemen, and children, in, practically, one room. For two nights I had a young married couple sleeping in the berth above mine. The lady turned in first, and presently her gown was hung out over the rail to which her bed curtains were fastened. But further processes of unrobing were indicated by the agitation of the drapery which concealed her nest. As the same curtain served for both berths – hers and mine – the gentleman held her portion together over my head when it was necessary for me to retire. At last all were housed, and some snores rose above the rattle of the train. I did not sleep much the first night, but looked over the moonlit prairie from my pillow.'

Although Pullman introduced a 'hotel car' in 1870 with a kitchen at one end from which meals were served on removable tables set between the drawing-room seats, the Union Pacific scheduled the car for only one trip each week. Until well into the 1880s the transcontinental railroad fed its passengers at dining stations along the way, allowing them thirty minutes to obtain their food and bolt it down before resuming the journey.

Judging from comments of travellers, the food varied from wretched to middling-fair. The first dining stop out of Omaha was Grand Island. 'Ill cooked and poorly served,' was one passenger's blunt comment. 'We found the quality on the whole bad,' said William Robertson of Scotland, 'and all three meals, breakfast, dinner and supper, were almost identical, viz., tea, buffalo steaks, antelope chops, sweet potatoes, and boiled Indian corn, with hoe cakes and syrup *ad nauseam*.' New Yorker Susan Coolidge also complained about the sameness of diet: 'It was necessary to look at one's watch to tell whether it was breakfast, dinner or supper that we were eating, these meals presenting invariably the same salient features of beefsteak, fried eggs, fried potato.' She was generous enough to compliment the chef at Sidney, Nebraska, for serving 'cubes of fried mush which diversified a breakfast of unusual excellence'. Harvey Rice of Cleveland, Ohio, described the Sidney breakfast station as a crude structure of boards and canvas. 'Here the passengers were replenished with an excellent breakfast – a chicken stew, as they supposed, but which, as they were afterwards informed, consisted of prairie-dogs – a new variety of chickens, without feathers. This information created an unpleasant sensation in sundry delicate stomachs.'

According to William L. Humason of Hartford, Connecticut, the farther one travelled across the plains, the worse the dining stations became, 'consisting of miserable shanties, with tables dirty, and waiters not only dirty, but saucy. The tea tasted as though it were made from the leaves of the sage-brush – literally *sage tea*. The biscuit was made without soda, but with plenty of alkali, harmonizing with the great quantity of alkali dust we had already swallowed.' The only dining station Humason had a good word for was at Cisco, California, where the water on the table was as clear as crystal, but he thought a dollar and a quarter was 'a pretty steep price to pay for fried ham and potatoes'.

At most dining stops, meal prices were one dollar, and on the California section of the Central Pacific the prices were reduced to seventy-five cents if the diner paid in silver rather than in paper money. Neither the Union Pacific nor the Central Pacific operated their eating houses, preferring to contract them to private individuals, with no required standard of service. Most of them were in rough frame buildings filled with long tables upon which large platters of food were waiting when passengers descended from the trains. Gradually the individual stations achieved reputations for certain specialities such as beefsteak at Laramie, hot biscuits at Green River, antelope at Sidney, fish at Colfax. The most frequently praised dining stop was Evanston, Wyoming, where mountain trout was the speciality. 'It was kept by a coloured man named Howard W. Crossley whose evident desire was to please all,' wrote John Lester. He added that most 'proprietors of the eating-stations ought to be promoted to higher callings; for they are evidently above running a hotel.'

Because Cheyenne was listed in the guidebooks as the largest city between Omaha and Sacramento, many passengers expected superior-quality food service there. They were disappointed to find a small town of board and canvas buildings occupied by about three thousand 'dangerous-looking miners in big boots, broad-brimmed hats, and revolvers'. The only added feature in the dining station was a formidable row of heads of big-game animals that glared down from the walls upon the famished passengers. 'The chops were generally as tough as hanks of whipcord, and the knives as blunt as bricklayers' trowels.' One traveller did mention favourably the antelope steaks served in Cheyenne, but Susan Coolidge was dubious, remarking that whenever beefsteak was unusually tough, the dining stations listed it as 'antelope' to give it the charm of novelty. She also noted that the rush of diners at Cheyenne was 'so great that you find it impossible to catch the eye of the Chinese waiter till it is too late to make him of the slightest use.' Before her journey ended she reached the conclusion that transcontinental travellers should pack lunch baskets; she recommended Albert biscuit, orange marmalade, fresh rolls, and cold roasted chicken, which could be obtained at Omaha and Ogden. Most male travellers, however, advised against lunch baskets, saying that they were always in the way and that the food was likely to spoil.

Between stops for meals, the passengers were diverted by a procession of unfamiliar wildlife along each side of the track, antelope and prairie dogs being the most commonly seen. Far more antelope than buffalo ranged along the Union Pacific tracks, and long files of these fleet-footed animals often approached very close to passing trains, 'apparently racing with the cars, and always winning in the race'. Although the Union Pacific frowned upon the practice, eager hunters sometimes fired upon these animals with rifles and pistols from the open windows of the cars. Few hits were recorded.

Prairie-dog villages also were close enough that passengers could observe these gregarious rodents sitting at the entrances to their burrows. 'They fling themselves in the air with a gay nimbleness beautiful to see, flip a somersault, and present to the admiring gaze of the traveller two furry heels and a short furry tail as they make their exit from the stage of action.'

Elk, wolves, and bears often were seen as the Iron Horse thundered across the West, and one traveller was sure that he saw a pack of wild dogs trotting along parallel to the railroad, until he learned that they were coyotes. Another unfamiliar sight were swarms of grasshoppers and crickets, which sometimes descended upon the tracks and caused the locomotive wheels to spin into a temporary stall.

Although only thinning herds of buffalo remained near the Union Pacific right-of-way after train travel began, the Iron Horses of the Kansas Pacific (less than two hundred miles to the south) occasionally were surrounded by buffalo and had to slow down or wait until the herd passed. One traveller on the Kansas Pacific told of seeing a herd that extended as far as the eye could reach. 'With heads down and tails up they galloped towards the track making extraordinary exertions to get across ahead of the locomotive. In trying this strategic feat one specimen found himself forcibly lifted into the air and thrown into the ditch, where he lay upon his back, his cloven feet flourishing madly.'

In its early days, before connections were scheduled with other railroads, the Kansas Pacific engineers willingly stopped trains to permit the passengers to leave the cars and shoot at passing buffalo. 'Everybody runs out and commences shooting,' lawyer John Putnam of Topeka wrote a friend in 1868. 'We failed to bag a buffalo. I did not shoot, having ill refined ideas as to hunting rifles, which end you put the load in and which end you let it out at ... But I rushed out with the rest – yelled promiscuously – "Buffalo! – Stop the train – let me out – there they are! – Whoop-pey – Give 'em thunder – no go – Come back – drive on" – So you see I helped a good deal.'

So eager was Randolph Keim of Washington, DC, to bag a buffalo from a train, he persuaded the engineer to let him ride up front on the Iron Horse. 'Taking my rifle I posted myself on the cow-catcher, or rather buffalo-catcher of the locomotive. After proceeding about ten miles, we struck a large herd crossing the track. The locomotive pursued its course without diminution of speed. Approaching the herd rather rapidly, I did not favor the idea of receiving a buffalo in my lap, a fact growing momentarily more probable. The herd had passed. One animal lagging in the rear out of bewilderment, or reckless daring, planted himself in the middle of the track, with his head down as much as to say, "Come on who ever you are and we'll try." As I felt no relish to be a party to any such cranial collision, and finding no other convenient place, took a conspicuous but uncomfortable position on the steamchest, holding on by the rail. I found the temperature as far as my feet were concerned anything but desirable, but in momentary anticipation of a rare display of buffalo meat, kept a sharp look-out for the pieces. At this moment, the whistle blew. The buffalo, startled at the shrill sound, made an effort to get out of the way. He succeeded, so far as to have his posteriors pretty well damaged, that is minus his tail, and to wind up with a series of acrobatic exercises over the embankment.'

The buffalo and other animals entertained the travellers against a constantly changing background of scenery that grew more and more fascinating as they left the plains behind. The first glimpse of the snowy range of the Rocky Mountains always sent a wave of excitement through the passenger cars. 'My boyish dreams were realized,' one man recorded. 'For hours, at the school desk, have I pondered over the map and wandered, in imagination, with Lewis and Clark, the hunters and trappers and early emigrants, away off to these Rocky Mountains, about which such a mystery seemed to hang, – dreaming, wishing and hoping against hope, that my eyes might, some day, behold their snow-crowned heights. And here lay the first great range in the pureness of white; distant, to be sure, but there it lay, enshrined in beauty.'

Wyoming was filled with wonders for these journeyers from the East, but when the Iron Horse brought them through tunnels into Utah's Echo and Weber canyons, they were at a loss for superlatives to describe the towering castle-like rocks. 'Grand beyond description ... castles in the air ... fantastic shapes and profiles ... the scene is as fearful as it is sublime.' Shortly after entering the narrows of Weber Canyon, virtually everyone made note of the Thousand-Mile Tree, a single green pine in a desolation of rock and sage, marking the distance from Omaha. European travellers compared Weber Canyon to gateways to the Alps. Castle Rock, Hanging Rock, Pulpit Rock, Devil's Gate, Devil's Slide – all entered the notebooks of scribbling travellers who seemed to disagree as to whether they were creations of God or of Satan.

Along the way were occasional reminders of pioneers of a previous day – the bones of long-dead oxen and horses beside the deep-rutted trails where covered wagons had crawled, a solitary grave marker, a broken wheel, a piece of discarded furniture. 'Inch by inch, the teams toiled to gain a higher foothold,' said one appreciative train traveller, 'inch by inch they *climbed* down the rugged passes; *now* in luxurious coaches, with horses of iron, with a skilled engineer for a driver we are carried along in comfort.'

When there were no animals or scenery to entertain or awe, there was always the ever-changing weather of the West. The train on which Harvey Rice was journeying to California in 1869 ran through a typically violent Great Plains thunderstorm. 'The heavens became, suddenly, as black as starless midnight. The lightning flashed in every direction, and electric balls of fire rolled over the plains. It seemed as if the artillery of heaven had made the valley a target and that we were doomed to instant destruction. But happily our fears were soon dissipated. The storm was succeeded by a brilliant rainbow.'

Heavy rains were likely to flood the tracks and in the early years before roadbeds were well ballasted, the ties sank into the mud. One traveller was startled to see the car behind him churning up such a foam of mud that it resembled a boat rushing along on water. It was not unusual for hailstorms to break car windows, and tornadoes could lift a train off the track. One of the legends of the Kansas Pacific concerns a tornadic waterspout that dropped out of a massive thunderstorm, washed out six thousand feet of track, and swallowed up a freight train. 'Although great efforts were made to find it,' said Charles B. George, a veteran railroad man, 'not a trace of it has ever been discovered.'

Winter travellers could expect magnificent snowstorms or fierce blizzards that sometimes turned a journey across the continent into an ordeal. On William Rae's return trip East from California in the winter of 1870, the Iron Horse pulling his train fought a two-hour battle with a snowstorm across four miles of the Laramie plains. The delay played havoc with train schedules on the single-track Union Pacific, but Rae reported that the hot-air stove in his Pullman car kept it 'as comfortable as the best-warmed room in an English house'.

Rae might not have been so fortunate had he been travelling on the Kansas Pacific, which suffered as severely from blizzards as it did from thunder squalls. High winds drifted both snow and sand into cuts, levelling them across the tops, and the sturdy little wood-burning locomotives would have to back up, be uncoupled from the cars, and then run at full speed into the snowbanked cuts. This was called 'bucking the snow', and usually had to be repeated several times before it was effective. Engineer Cy Warman told of bucking an eighteen-foot drift with double engines so hard that his locomotive trembled and shook as if it were about to be crushed into pieces. 'Often when we came to a stop only the top of the stack of the front engine would be visible ... All this time the snow kept coming down, day and night, until the only signs of a railroad across the range were the tops of the telegraph poles.' If the passengers were lucky, the train was backed to the nearest station, but even then conditions might be harsh. A group of snowbound train travellers who crowded into a hotel in Hays City, Kansas, spent an uncomfortably cold night and at daylight found their beds covered with snow that had drifted through cracks in walls and roof.

The universal desire of all pioneer travellers on the transcontinental was to see a 'real wild Indian'. Few of them did, because the true warriors of the plains hated the Iron Horse and seldom came within miles of it. After the resisting tribes finally realized they could not stop the building of the Union Pacific's iron tracks, their leaders signed treaties that removed their people from the broad swaths of land taken by the railroad. As the buffalo herds also fled far to the north and south, there was no economic reason for the horse Indians to approach the railroad. The Indians whom the travellers saw were mostly those who had been corrupted and weakened by contacts with the white man's civilization – scroungers, mercenaries, or beggars by necessity.

Except for a few acculturated representatives of Mississippi Valley tribes (who still plaited their hair but wore white man's clothing and frequented railroad stations from Chicago to Omaha), the westbound travellers' first glimpse of Plains Indians was around the Loup Fork in Nebraska, where the Pawnees lived on a reservation. Although the Pawnees had virtually abandoned their horse-buffalo culture and lived off what they could cadge from white men, the warriors still shaved their heads to a tuft, painted their faces, and wore feathers and blankets. To travellers fresh from the East, the Pawnees had a very bloodthirsty appearance, and according to the guidebooks every one of them had several scalps waving from the tops of lodgepoles.

Anywhere across western Nebraska or Wyoming, a traveller might catch a quick glimpse of a passing Sioux, Cheyenne, Arapaho, or Crow staring at the Iron Horse, but they were few and far between. Not until the train reached Nevada was there a plenitude of Shoshonis and Paiutes hanging about every station and using their treaty rights with the Central Pacific to ride the cars back and forth. Because these desert Indians were generally covered with dust and were often unbathed because there was no water readily available, the fastidious passengers found them objectionable, and the Central Pacific gradually put restrictions on their use of trains. At first they were confined to the emigrants' coaches, and then after the emigrants objected to their presence, the Indians had to ride in the baggage cars or outside on the boarding steps.

'We were regaled with the sight, for the first time, of a group of wild Indians,' a traveller noted at one of the Nevada stations. 'Some of the squaws were burdened with papooses strapped to their backs. They expected and received a "shower" of donations from the passengers in the shape of "cold victuals" and "silver quarters". This made them happy. Among them were some of the finest specimens of physical manhood that I ever saw.' The Indian women soon discovered that the travellers on the trains were so eager to see the infants snuggled in their basket cradles that they could command from ten cents to a quarter in exchange for a look inside.

Lady Duffus Hardy was frankly more interested in the handsome males who were loading wood into the locomotive tender. 'One especially attracted our attention ... He wore a blue blanket wrapped around him, and on his head a broad-brimmed ragged felt hat with a mass of blue feathers drooping on his shoulders. The men stood in groups, solemnly regarding us with their big black eyes, still as statues; the women squatted on the platform or peeped at us from round corners. It was not exactly pleasant, but very interesting to find ourselves amid a score or two of this savage race, the men all armed with guns and knives.'

Other travellers spent a considerable amount of time worrying about what the warlike Indians might do if they put their minds to it. 'It would be an easy matter,' wrote an apprehensive New Englander, 'for them to rush on to an unprotected portion of the road, in the night, tear up the track, withdraw until the train comes up, is thrown from the track, or brought to a standstill, then rush forward again, and tear up the track in the rear of the cars, and thus have all the passengers at their mercy.' After brooding on these possibilities, he added complacently: 'The poor Indian has few friends, and his days will soon be numbered.'

Such perturbed passengers might better have been fretting over Anglo-Saxon train robbers, such as Jesse James, who were far more likely to wreck and rob a train in the 1870s than were the Indians. Only eighteen months after the rails were joined at Promontory, a gang of six robbers quietly boarded the eastbound Central Pacific express at Truckee, California. An hour later, at one-thirty in the morning on 5 November 1870, the train stopped at Verdi, Nevada, to take on fuel and water. Just as the engineer got his locomotive rolling again, one of the robbers dropped down from the tender into the cab, pointed a pair of pistols at the engineer and fireman, and ordered them to stop the train. At this point his five companions jumped from the first coach, uncoupled it from the express car, and a few seconds later the engine and express car with the six robbers aboard were moving rapidly away in the darkness.

With smooth efficiency the robbers broke in upon the unsuspecting express agent and took the entire Virginia City payroll – more than forty thousand dollars. After the robbers left the express car, the engineer backed his abbreviated train nine miles to Verdi, where a bewildered conductor was waiting with several cars of sleeping passengers, few of whom were aware of what had happened. This was the first robbery of a Central Pacific train, an act that was repeated only twenty-four hours later on the same train, four hundred miles farther east near Toano, Nevada. The second haul was almost as large as the first. After that, Wells Fargo Express assigned armed guards to valuable shipments; nevertheless, holdups continued for many years on the Central Pacific and its successor, the Southern Pacific.

Evidently the Union Pacific kept a tighter security on its express shipments. The first robbery on that line did not occur until 27 August 1875, near Bitter Creek, Wyoming, when two inept bandits entered a moving express car through an unbarred window. They found the express agent asleep, but instead of seizing and tying him up they tried to filch his keys from his pocket. This awoke him, of course, and in the melee that followed, several wild shots were fired, the expressman pulled the bell cord to signal the engineer to stop, and the robbers grabbed up armloads of packages and fled. They were not caught, but all they had gained for their efforts were a few articles of little value.

Three years later, Big Nose George Parrot and Dutch Charlie Burris decided to derail a Union Pacific payroll train near Rawlins, Wyoming. They loosened a rail on a curve and waited hopefully in a nearby willow thicket. As luck would have it, a railroad section boss chose that afternoon to make a walking inspection of the track. When he observed the freshly drawn spikes lying beside the loose rail, he read their meaning instantly.

Suspecting that would-be train robbers were in the vicinity, he pretended not to have seen anything, until he was out of sight around the curve. Then he ran as fast as he could until he saw the train approaching and flagged it to a stop. He learned afterwards that the robbers had their rifles trained on him; Big Nose George started to put a bullet in the track walker's back, but because the man did not even break his stride at the loosened rail he held his fire. A posse was soon in pursuit, but the bandits killed two of the deputies and escaped to Montana. Not until several months later were they captured, and while they were being returned to Rawlins for trial, an angry mob invaded the train on which they were riding, seized Dutch Charlie, and hanged him from a telegraph pole. The sheriff managed to get Big Nose George into a jail, but when rumours spread that the bandit had made an attempt to escape, another gang of vigilantes broke into the jail and hanged Big Nose George.

The robber whom railroad passengers most feared was Jesse James, and the very first train that Jesse robbed was carrying a load of transcontinental travellers – on the Rock Island line between Adair and Council Bluffs, Iowa, on the evening of 21 July 1873. The James boys loosened a rail, tied a rope to it, and when the train came rumbling into view they jerked the rail clear of the track. The locomotive plunged over on its side, killing the engineer, and a number of passengers were injured in the derailed cars. While some of the bandits entered the express car, others marched through the coaches, robbing the startled travellers of their money and watches and jewellery. They were on their horses riding hellbent for the Missouri hills before train crew or passengers fully realized what had happened to them.

Not all train wrecks signalled an invasion by robbers, however, and because of the relatively slow speeds of the early years, bruises rather than fatalities were the likely results, unless the accident occurred on a high bridge or mountain shoulder. Poor tracks and hot boxes (overheating of axle bearings) caused many wrecks, and a surprising number of passengers suffered injuries from falling or jumping out of open car windows. One of the pioneer passengers of 1869 recorded how it felt to be in a train wreck in Echo Canyon: 'On we bounded over the ties, the car wheels breaking many of them as though they were but pipe-stems. Every instant we expected to roll down the ravine. We ordered the ladies to cling to the sides of the seats and keep their feet clear of the floor. It seemed as if that train could never be stopped! But it was brought to a standstill upon the brink of an embankment. Had the cars gone a few rods further the reader would probably never have been troubled by these hastily written pages.'

Still another westbound traveller during that first year told of being shaken out of his seat when a Central Pacific train ran into a herd of cattle between Wadsworth and Clark's Station, Nevada. The collision threw the locomotive off the track, but a telegrapher aboard climbed the nearest pole, tapped the line, and summoned a relief engine. During the eight-hour delay the hungry but resourceful passengers butchered the dead cattle, built a fire, and cooked steaks. Such encounters with cattle were among the most common causes of train wrecks in the West, and railroad men and ranchers were in constant friction for more than half a century over the rights of cattle to trespass upon railroad property.

Within a few weeks after the transcontinental railroad began operations, a flood of guidebooks for travellers appeared for sale in all the main terminals. Crofutt's, Appleton's, and Williams' were among the most popular, each publisher issuing several series. H. Wallace Atwell, who signed himself 'Bill Dadd, the Scribe', led the Crofutt entries with his *Great Trans-Continental Railroad Guide*. George Crofutt claimed that he sold half a million copies of his guides during the 1870s in spite of competition from numerous imitators.

Anyone familiar with the melodramatic fiction of the nineteenth century can easily detect a similarity between the style of the dime novels, or penny dreadfuls, and that of many contemporary railroad guides. Possibly the same hack writers worked in both fields, applying the myths of the American West to that region's railroads. The guidebook writers could not resist overplaying the wickedness of Julesburg and other Hell on Wheels towns. They lingered upon the gamblers and painted ladies, included lengthy accounts of such characters as Blacksnake Lachut, who could cut a man to pieces with his long whip, and amused himself in dance halls by flicking off the buttons that held up the straps of the dancing girls' dresses. Some guidebook writers implied that wild orgies were still constant occurrences in the former Hell on Wheels towns, although in reality little more than a water tank might remain. Even so, imaginative passengers peering from their car windows revelled in the guidebook iniquities of Julesburg, Benton, or Corinne, and scribbled in their own notebooks that 'thieves, gamblers, cut-throats and prostitutes stalked brazen-faced in broad day through the streets.' Walt Whitman also must have read the guidebooks, refining the dross into gold in his *Passage to India*. His account of a journey West on the Pacific railroad contains traces of guidebook phrases woven into his reverberating lines.

Thanks to energetic photographers and lecturers and the development of the magic lantern, it was possible to experience the thrills of Western railroad travel vicariously, without ever leaving one's home in Manhattan, Queens, Long Island, Connecticut, or New Jersey – these being the places where 'Professor' Stephen James Sedgwick earned a handsome income during the 1870s by taking his audiences on lantern slide tours of the transcontinental railroad.

Sedgwick was a New York schoolteacher who had toyed with the magic lantern as an instructional aid, and then in the late 1860s after a gas and calcium device made it possible to project brilliant limelight pictures onto a screen for large audiences, the 'Professor' abandoned his classroom and became the leading exhibitor of 'lantern' shows in churches, schools, and public halls throughout the East. For almost a decade, he projected the marvellously detailed photographs of Andrew J. Russell, William Henry Jackson, Charles R. Savage, Alfred Hart, and C. E. Watkins, skilfully arranging his glass slides so that at the end of one of his lectures his audience felt as if they truly had travelled by rail to the Western Sea. These were motionless pictures, of course, but from his first slide of Russell's brilliant shot of the entrance to the Missouri River bridge, the trusses and girders of which magically drew its viewers into the infinity of the West, through hundreds of scenes of towns and bridges and mountains, alternating close-ups with long shots, Sedgwick forced a sense of movement into his imaginary journeys. Supported by the reality of the camera, Sedgwick in his lectures added to the general illusion of the American West, 'the preordained home' of a people chosen by manifest destiny, hailing the builders of the railroad as noble patriots all, the Pacific being the goal of empire.

What influence Sedgwick had upon train travel to the West cannot be measured. Undoubtedly many members of his audiences were inspired to make the real journey, coming to it with a sense of prejudgment, of induced paramnesia. The scribblers among them also surely read the dime-novel guidebooks, and with a strange gullibility adopted the attitudes of the popular culture of the times, lifting entire paragraphs directly out of the cheapest paperbacks. Numerous published travel accounts of the period are permeated with guidebook legends; for example, one of the most frequently copied statements concerned the town of Wahsatch: 'Out of twenty-four graves here, but one holds the remains of a person who died a natural death – and she was a prostitute who poisoned herself.' Even that honest reporter, John Beadle, borrowed the story, increasing the number of graves to forty-three and doubling the suicides. Yet, it was not so much fictionalized 'facts' that influenced readers of the guidebooks, it was the fictionalized attitudes. They swallowed the guidebooks' stories of dangers from wild Indians, lurid accounts that usually ended with a paragraph of solemn advice to buy travel insurance. This might have led cynical travellers to wonder if the publishers of guidebooks were also in the insurance business, but the reaction was more likely to be that of one reader of *Appleton's Handbook of American Travel* who asked himself: 'If pleasure travelling in the United States be regarded as fraught with so much danger, is it not wiser to stay at home?'

Sophisticated travellers such as William Rae did challenge the guidebooks that assured him that at certain stops he could see Long's Peak and Pike's Peak. 'It is possible that these mountain tops may have been discerned in a vision by the compilers of guidebooks,' he said. 'To the eye of the ordinary and unimaginative traveller they are invisible.' Rae was also caustic about a guidebook's description of the Dale Creek bridge. 'The grandest feature of the road,' the guidebook author wrote enthusiastically, praising the bridge for its 'light, airy, and graceful appearance'.

Rae commented that he preferred to lose a fine sight rather than risk a broken neck, and added that he did not breathe freely until the cars had passed safely over the rickety bridge.

The guides occasionally offered useful advice, especially for women who had little idea of what they would need on such a long journey. In addition to the usual baggage, it was suggested that a small valise be carried for a night-dress, clean collars and cuffs, pocket-handkerchiefs and stockings, a bottle of cologne, a vial of powdered borax to soften the Western water, a warm flannel sack for chilly nights, a whisk broom, a pocket pin cushion, a brandy flask, and two linen dusters. On leaving Omaha, another guide recommended, a lady should wear a light spring suit; on the second day as the train approached the Rockies, change to a winter suit was suggested. On the third day across Utah and the Nevada desert, she should don a summer suit, and then on the fourth day in the Sierras, the winter suit and 'all your underclothing' would be required. The fifth and last day of course would bring her into sunny California and the summer suit again.

Bill Dadd, the Scribe, was less considerate in his attitude towards women travellers: 'It is not right or just for a *lady* to occupy one whole seat with her flounces and herself, and another with her satchel, parasol, big box, little box, bandbox and bundle, as we have often seen them do, while plain-dressed, hard-handed toiling men are obliged to remain standing in the crowded car. The woman who indulges in such flights of fancy as to suppose that one fare entitles her to monopolize three seats should not travel until bloomers come in fashion.' Another guidebook gravely pondered the question of whether the male or female of a couple travelling together should take the window seat. In the more civilized Eastern states, proper etiquette gave the seat to the woman, but in the unrefined West where both animals and human beings performed their natural functions in the open, it was decided that the man should occupy the window seat so that if the occasion arose he could shield the view outside from his lady.

At times on the journey, said Henry Williams in *The Pacific Tourist*, one should 'sit and read, play games, and indulge in social conversation and glee.' By 'glee' the guidebook author probably was referring to the improvised musicales and recitations that were especially popular among the Pullman passengers. In the early 1870s some Pullman cars had organs installed on them, and in the evenings amateur musicians as well as professional travelling troupes willingly gave performances. 'Music sounds upon the prairie and dies away far over the plains; merry-making and jokes, conversation and reading pass the time pleasantly until ten o'clock, when we retire ... If people who are travelling together will only try to make those about them happy, then a good time is assured. The second night on the road we arranged a little entertainment in the car and invited the ladies and gentlemen from the other cars into our "improvised Music Hall". The exercises consisted principally of recitations, with the delineation of the characters of Grace Greenwood ... The young ladies sang for us; and we were all happy – for the time at least.'

It was customary on Sundays to hold religious services in one of the cars. On a train rolling through western Wyoming in 1872, John Lester read the Episcopal service, the Reverend Mr Murray delivered a sermon entitled 'To Die Is Gain', and a choir sang 'Nearer, My God, to Thee' and the American national hymn. 'Here in the very midst of the Rocky Mountain wilderness,' wrote Lester, 'our thanksgivings were offered up; and our music floated out upon the air, and resounded through the deep caverns, and among the towering hills.'

According to most travellers, the popular diversions were cards, conversations, and reading. 'We had an abundant supply of books and newspapers. A boy frequently traversed the train with a good store of novels, mostly English, periodicals, etc.... In the evening we had our section lighted, and played a solemn game of whist, or were initiated into the mysteries of euchre, or watching the rollicking game of poker being carried on by a merry party in the opposite section.'

There may have been some 'rollicking' poker games on Pullman cars, but most of them were as deadly serious as the real money-making endeavours of the players in that Gilded Age of the Robber Barons. Brakeman Harry French told of witnessing such a game one evening in the course of his duties. 'The car was loaded to capacity with wealthy stockmen, and I suspect, a number of fancy women. In the cramped quarters of the men's smoking room, a high-play poker game was in progress. Gold pieces and bills were the stakes, and they were very much in evidence. I was particularly interested in one of the players. Fine clothes, careful barbering, diamond-decked fingers marked him as a gambler.' Poker-playing professional gamblers, fresh from the declining riverboat traffic of the Mississippi River, could indeed be found on almost any transcontinental train in the 1870s, and many a greenhorn bound West to seek his fortune lost his nest egg before reaching the end of his journey.

As in any era, travellers found plenty of entertainment in merely observing their fellow passengers. 'It was curious to see a rough-booted, broad-brimmed fellow strutting up and down the train with his revolver slung behind him like a short blunt tail,' said the London Parson. 'But, of course, if you leave them alone they don't meddle with you. They only shoot their friends and acquaintances, as a rule.' Travellers from abroad were repelled by the widespread American habit of chewing tobacco (coaches and Pullmans were furnished with an ample supply of brass cuspidors), but by the time they crossed the continent they grew accustomed to seeing fellow passengers expelling fountains of tobacco juice, and to sharing seats with burly miners who boarded the train with pockets full of tobacco plugs and whisky bottles, which they were eager to share with their seat mates. 'Smile?' a dusty-bearded Westerner might say to a well-dressed traveller, and the latter soon understood that 'Smile?' was mining-country slang for 'Have a drink?' The farther west the train rolled, the rougher and more unrestrained the local passengers became. 'A fiercer, hirsute, and unwashed set I never saw,' said one Easterner, 'but for my part I found them pleasant companions, under the circumstances.'

By the time the train reached Sherman Summit on the second day out of Omaha, the passengers had formed into the usual little groups and cliques, and knew one another by sight if not by name. Sherman Summit, the most elevated station on the Pacific railroad (the highest in the world, according to the guide-books) was also the halfway point between Omaha and the Union Pacific's end of track at Ogden. If the westbound express was on schedule, the engineer would stop his panting Iron Horse longer than usual at the Sherman water tank in order to give the passengers a chance to stretch their legs, inhale the rarefied air, and enjoy the view before crossing Dale Creek bridge and plunging down the mountains into Laramie for a noon meal stop.

At Sherman, some passengers were afflicted with nose bleed from the height, or were badly chilled by the cold wind, and were glad to leave it behind. Others found it inspiring: 'Never till this moment did I realize the truthfulness of Bierstadt's scenery of these hills. The dark, deep shadows, the glistening sides, and the snow-capped peaks, with their granite faces, the stunted growth of pine and cedar, all render the scene such as he has painted it.' And another traveller, Dr H. Buss, whose medical skills may have been better than his poetry, preserved the memory of his visit in verse:

Now, Sherman on the Rocky Mountain range,
   Eight thousand feet is raised towards the sky,
Indian, Chinese, and many people strange,
   Are met or passed as o'er the earth you fly.

After lunch at Laramie, where 'the people around the station are more intelligent-looking than at any place since leaving Omaha', the train was soon across Medicine Bow River and into Carbon Station, where coal had been discovered and was rapidly replacing wood for fuel on the Union Pacific locomotives. Westbound travellers usually crossed Wyoming's deserts after nightfall, but even by moonlight the endless sweep of dry sagebrush and greasewood was described by various travellers as dreary, awful, lifeless. They complained of burning eyes and sore lips caused by the clouds of alkali dust swirled up into the cars, and thought Bitter Creek and Salt Wells were appropriately descriptive names for stations.

About sunrise the train arrived at Green River for a breakfast stop, and for the next hundred miles everyone looked forward to the moment of crossing into Utah Territory, the land of the Mormons and their plural wives. Wahsatch was the noon dining station, and every passenger from the East who stepped down from the train peered expectantly around for Mormons, but the

What Cheer Eating House looked about the same as all the others they had seen.

A group of passengers from New England who were travelling on one of the first trains to the West in 1869 were delayed by bad tracks near Wahsatch and had to spend the night there. 'What a place to stop in! No buildings – nothing but tents or shanties, and all of them "whisky hells" of the lowest kinds. We worked our way through the most villainous-looking crowd that man ever yet set eyes on, to an old sleeping car on a discontinued sidetrack, which proved to be densely populated with "creeping things".' Wahsatch was filled with several hundred discharged railroad construction workers who had just been paid off by Dr Durant after the 'capture' of his private car, and they were noisily spending their money.

'We were afraid they would attack our sleeping car and "go through it" as the phrase is, and rob the passengers. The ladies were very much frightened; there was very little sleep in the car that night. The doors were securely locked. Some of the party had arms and stood on guard. Many times in the night some of the "roughs" attempted to get in, and were driven away. They were apparently too drunk to form any organized plan of assault. I did not sleep, and shall long remember those sounds that made the night hideous, of howling, cursing, swearing and pistol shots. Fights occurred by the score; we could distinctly hear the blows. Knives were freely used, and the stabbing affrays were numerous. One man was shot directly under our car windows.'

About fifty miles farther west, after passing through Echo and Weber canyons, was Uintah Station, a connecting point for Wells Fargo stagecoaches to Salt Lake City. As it was almost de rigueur for transcontinental travellers to visit the Mormon capital, numerous passengers endured the rough thirty-mile stage journey. The jarring and jolting was enough 'to beat a man into a jelly or to break every bone in his body ... I am amazed that the wheels and framework of the coach remained unbroken and unstrained.' After the rail spur line from Ogden to Salt Lake City was completed early in 1870, the pilgrimage to the City of the Saints was much easier. When Lady Hardy discovered that the conductor on her train from Ogden was a Mormon, she immediately asked him how many wives he had. She was disillusioned by his polite reply that he had only one. She had been under the false impression that polygamy was imposed by the church and that all Mormon men had several wives.

Salt Lake City was a revelation to all Easterners whose heads had been filled with anti-Mormon propaganda. 'The city, in point of wealth and beauty, far exceeded my expectations,' wrote one. 'It is a perfect Eden.' Another described it as 'an oasis in a desert, a blooming garden in a wilderness of green.' Almost everyone was entranced by the streams of sparkling water that flowed along the sides of the broad streets, melted snow brought down from the surrounding mountains to irrigate fields and gardens. Harvey Rice, who arrived there in September 1869, found ripened fruit hanging from tree limbs over the sidewalks in front of almost every cottage. The Englishman William Rae admired the extreme purity of the atmosphere, but was annoyed by the flies in the dining room of the highly touted Townsend House, which catered to these early tourists. A Finnish baroness, Alexandra Gripenberg, said the Mormons 'had done a good piece of work in Utah', and admired their endurance in transforming a desert into a garden.

Few travellers, however, could resist criticizing the beliefs of Brigham Young and his followers, although those who met Young – who seemed never to refuse interviews – usually came away admiring him for his frankness and abilities. 'He exhibited a degree of refinement and intelligence in his discourse which surprised me,' said Harvey Rice, who decided to overlook the faults of the Mormons because they were 'a quiet, orderly people'. By the time the transcontinental travellers were back in Uintah or Ogden to resume their journeys to the Pacific, almost all had revised their opinions of a people who at that time were generally depicted in popular print as depraved fanatics with no redeeming qualities.

At Ogden, passengers awaiting connecting trains frequently had to spend many hours in a long narrow wooden building that had been erected between the tracks of the Union Pacific and the Central Pacific. In addition to ticket offices and a large dining room, sleeping rooms furnished only with curtains for doors were available upstairs. Lady Hardy considered her enforced stay there an adventure: 'Except for the passing trains this is a most lonely, isolated spot, weird and still, lying in the heart of the mountains. In the evening a blinding snowstorm came on, and the wind, howling fearfully with a rushing mighty sound, shook the doors and rattled at the windows as though it wanted to come in and warm itself at our blazing wood fire.'

Upon boarding the Central Pacific at Ogden, the first-class passengers found themselves in Silver Palace cars instead of Pullmans. Collis Huntington and his Big Four partners refused to accept George Pullman's arrangement for the use of his sleeping cars and ordered their own constructed. The Silver Palaces were attractive with their white metallic interiors, and although they were outfitted with private sitting rooms and smoking rooms, they lacked the luxurious touches that travellers from the East had grown accustomed to in their Pullmans. Passengers complained that their berths were not as roomy or as comfortable, and some said the cars were often too cold. Eventually the Central Pacific had to give up the Silver Palaces because transcontinental passengers resented having to change from their Pullmans.

The earliest experiment in running a Pullman train from coast to coast was conducted in the spring of 1870 by affluent members of the Boston Board of Trade. Participating in the event was George Pullman himself, along with 129 members of such leading families of Boston as the Rices, Peabodys, Danas, Warrens, Farwells, Houghtons, and Whitneys. The Pullman Hotel Express consisted of two sleeping cars, two hotel cars, a commissary car, dining car, smoking car, and baggage car. The smoking car was divided into four compartments, one outfitted for publication of a daily newspaper, *The Trans-Continental*, another with tables for card games, a wine room, and a barber shop. The baggage car not only carried the party's luggage and several chests of ice, it also contained a large flask of symbolic water from the Atlantic Ocean. As added complements to this prototype of luxurious trains of the future, Pullman included two libraries and two organs.

Amid a considerable amount of newspaper publicity, the Pullman Hotel Express crossed the continent in seven days (it stopped